IN SEARCH
OF SELF

IN SEARCH OF SELF

Reflections from the Eastern Caribbean

MARY ANN BACHMAN KOLLENBERG

ARCHWAY PUBLISHING

Archway Publishing books may be ordered through booksellers or by contacting:

Archway Publishing
1663 Liberty Drive
Bloomington, IN 47403
www.archwaypublishing.com
1 (888) 242-5904

Because of the dynamic nature of the Internet, any web addresses or links contained in this book may have changed since publication and may no longer be valid. The views expressed in this work are solely those of the author and do not necessarily reflect the views of the publisher, and the publisher hereby disclaims any responsibility for them.

Any people depicted in stock imagery provided by Thinkstock are models, and such images are being used for illustrative purposes only.
Certain stock imagery © Thinkstock.

ISBN: 978-1-4808-1667-1 (sc)
ISBN: 978-1-4808-1668-8 (e)

Library of Congress Control Number: 2015904355

Print information available on the last page.

Archway Publishing rev. date: 05/05/2015

Author and Marge at Scott's Head 1993

Preface

It's How You See It
By: Mary Ann Kollenberg, Dominica

Almost since the day I began Peace Corps Training on St. Lucia in mid-July 1992, I've written home to family and friends, sharing with them, my numerous Peace Corps experiences and a range of personal feelings. In early October I received a letter from a special friend who wrote:

"More than ever before you seem to have a better "comfort" level with Peace Corps, Dominica, and Portsmouth - finally getting Used to the fact that it is 'OK' not to witness tangible progress every day as you're accustomed to in ordinary life. Yours is a gift of 'love' more than a gift of 'labor,' and love is not as measurable as labor."

Need more be said?

Looking North toward Roseau, September 1993

July 15, 1992 - St. Lucia

Dear Family and Friends:

Today I finished my first day of official Peace Corps Training. Keep in mind I'm only a PC Trainee until I successfully pass training and am sworn in as a True Volunteer on the Island of Dominica on August 19.

Training exposes us to many things: language, culture, Peace Corps rules and regulations, PC staff who are working in the Eastern Caribbean, personal safety, technical training and SHOTS!

In Miami, where we had three days of orientation called staging, we each got a yellow fever shot, a measles and mumps booster, and a polio booster. Here on St. Lucia we are being treated to a diphtheria and tetanus shot, a T.B. test, and a gamma globulin test for hepatitis A. All the volunteers going to Grenada will also get two shots for rabies! Rumor has it that all the dogs on Grenada are rabid. Such a morbid detail.

Two fellows from Dominica were part of the training staff for today's session. They told us over and over how green Dominica was, how you could drink the water right from the tap, and how Dominica has so much water it exports it to the other islands!

Those of us (12 in number) who have been blessed with a Dominica assignment feel we are by far the most fortunate and best group in the bunch. And that is just a great feeling.

I sound full of self-confidence, but the confidence does waver at times. Just like this a.m. following a fitful night's sleep and leaving Miami at 9:00 a.m. on Tuesday which meant rising at 4:00 a.m., flying to San Juan, Puerto Rico, then on to St. Lucia, followed by a 1 ½ hour drive around the island to Castries only to get caught in the 4:00 traffic! (It's as bad as Highway 49!) After an hour getting through this beautiful town to our meeting spot, we were greeted by local Peace Corps people and assigned a homestay family. It took another hour to get luggage and all together. But we did!

My host family Julian and Madaleine Gustave and their two children, Hermia (14) and Jervan (19 months) treat me like a queen. Hermia hangs on every word I say, and Jervan looks at me with his huge brown eyes and tries to mimic my oohs and ahhs. He is a livewire and needs to be watched every moment. The house has been "child-proofed" for saner living. The family is Seventh Day Adventist, very nice and so polite. Julian is a pest control man and Madaleine is a high school English teacher. They have welcomed me into the family. Madaleine who first learned to teach at age 15, was taught by the Peace Corps.

They live in a nice house about ½ hour out of Castries in an agricultural area. The community is called simply Hill 20. All of us going to Dominica have been placed in homes where we can learn French-Creole and experience a culture similar to Dominica.

I can't even begin to explain the roads or the drivers. It is all left-hand side. Many people get around by public transportation which consists of numerous 12-passenger vans that whiz here and there, up hills, along narrow streets, around corners that horseback riders would explore before venturing forth, their horns beeping at friends, other vans, blind corners and walkers who may not get out of the way.

The rain is beating on the roof again and I'll have to continue tomorrow. July 16. Each day so many things happen and almost wipe out the experience of the previous day. I feel I must write every day and do in my journal, but most of that you'll never see.

Today my host sister Hermia and I rode the bus to Castries at 8:00 a.m. We got off in downtown Castries and walked over a mile to the training building. Hermia took me through the market and along the side streets and main streets, along a harbor, through the mud and across the cracked sidewalks. The buildings have much charm. They are painted many colors and seem smaller than American buildings. Many have verandas at street level. There is an open ditch that runs alongside the sidewalks. It is concrete like the walk and carries all manner of interesting looking grey, often foul, water. But it doesn't seem to bother, possibly because it is the rainy season and as such, the hot sun does not beat down on it all day long.

We walk in pairs or with many people. It is still too early to even think of walking alone. At home on Hill 20, the winding narrow road hugs the canyon edge and lets the walker look out over brilliant green valleys across to other ridges and hills. As far as the eyes can see are banana trees, plantain, mango, breadfruit, guava, and avocado, pear, and coconut trees. My host family squeezes fresh juice for me each night as a dessert. We've eaten five kinds of potatoes, all delicious and with their own individual flavor – some sweet, some salty, all fixed very plain.

There is drama in Peace Corps life just like home – one girl has a bad, bad case of poison ivy and can't attend training. She evidently picked it up on her last day in the States. She is from upstate New York and had a party the day before she left. She thinks she ran in the woods to chase the volleyball. Another lady, Beth, who is planning to go to Dominica, received an emergency call today that her mother had gotten very ill!

It is hard enough just coping with all the change and newness and all the work we must do, let alone having to face other major problems!

Riding home on the transport (bus) today, I felt so carefree! As I bounced from hard spot to hard spot, I thought I wouldn't be doing this at home! Here I was all dressed up (the Prime Minister and East Caribbean Ambassador from the U.S. spoke at opening ceremonies for Peace Corps today). We were required to look our best. We also had photos taken. But here I was at 5:30 p.m. squashed in a 12-passenger van (made in Japan) with about 15 other sweaty, dripping bodies, the radio or tape blaring Reggae (Calypso) music, and the driver whipping around corners while passengers waved or yelled hellos to their friends along the route. And me, I had not a care in the world. It was such a marvelous feeling I just began to laugh and shared my thoughts with another P.C. trainee.

I am comfortable in my host family's home. I love the other trainees: they are all special and from all over the U.S. – California has the most. Our training is hard and takes all day every day except Saturday and Sunday. We do many small, interactive activities during training and are getting to know each other very well. I'm already planning my stateside visits to different locations when I get out! Just kidding!

There are three geckos outside my window this evening, and a frog hopped along the path on our walk this evening – but that's been the extent of my wildlife viewing – which is fine with me at this point. The "younger" crowd is planning a trek to the beach after training tomorrow followed by a go at a Friday night Jump-Up. Maybe I can explain that term later.

Mail evidently takes about eight days to reach St. Lucia. My address here is:

PC Trainee Mary Ann Kollenberg
PCEC
Box 123 American Drywall Building
Castries
St. Lucia, West Indies
My address after August 17 will be:
PC Volunteer Mary Ann Kollenberg
PC – Dominica
18 Bath Road
Roseau, Dominica

My telephone number from now until August 17th is 450-5183. Please share your letter with anyone who might be interested. Thank you all for the party! It was a lovely sendoff and I've brought photos with me.

Love, Mary Ann
P.S. Your support is with me every day!

July 26, 1992 - St Lucia 9:00 p.m. Sunday

Dear Mom and Bill:

My plan is to send you two pages with this letter and two more in a few days. If you could type up these pages if you wish to, but don't send any out until you get all four of my pages. Actually, if I write on both sides it will be eight total. I haven't settled on a workable system for letter writing yet, but I'm sure it will come easier once I'm on Dominica in my own place.

Also, I've discovered you had better send me back a copy of what I wrote so I'll know not to repeat myself next time. It seems, here in this lazy world, I forget what I've written about. I'm looking forward to hearing from you.

Love, MA
Again, the spelling help is appreciated!

July 26, 1992 – St. Lucia

Dear Family and Friends:

I was so anxious to write to you last time and so anxious to tell you I'd arrived safely that I forgot to thank you all for the support and encouragement you've offered me throughout the Peace Corps process. You have no idea how many times the thought of each of you crosses my mind. I've now been here long enough to miss the grandchildren, Josh, Kyle and Kayla. Lori tells me Kayla can sit up! By now she can probably crawl.

Just in case you might be curious – the Peace Corps process is still occurring. We 64 (-2) new recruits have been treated to a session on Peace Corp Policy by the Peace Corps Director, an ex-volunteer. I think he served 20 years ago on Haiti. The biggest arm of Peace Corps seems to be the medical. We are still being shot, talked to, and given material we are expected to read. Our latest is a book called <u>Where There is No Doctor</u>. I don't know if I mentioned the medical kit. Each one (and we each get one) weighs five pounds, and contains everything from Gatorade to aspirin and a thermometer. We even have sore throat lozenges, Tums (under another name) foot powder and a first-aid handbook!

The Peace Corps is a bureaucracy and don't let anyone tell you different. They, of course, are the first to admit it! I'm very curious about the level of service and training once we get "on Island," as they say in P.C. jargon. Here in St. Lucia we are hovered over and made to believe the attention standard will remain. Somehow, I doubt it (and hope I'm right), because Dominica is without a Country Director at present. One of the St. Lucia P.C. staff is stepping in until a new one can be hired.

It seems the lady Country Director who just left, Mary Ann by name, was extremely well liked and was able to get some very good environmental programs and projects begun on Dominica. The feeling is, she'll be missed! She left the warmth of the E.C. for the Ukraine in Russia. From not even sheets at night to fur-lined underwear!

July 27, 1992 - St Lucia

Good morning. It is now 10:30 a.m. (7:30 your time), and we've just finished a Community Training Session. I'm my own until a 2:30 appointment in Castries at the OECS (Office of Eastern Caribbean States). A good part of our training is "hands on." We are to learn all about the agencies that will be involved in our projects. So instead of being told, we locate the agency and go there for interviews. My vocational education background is proving invaluable!

Today I'll go to the OECS, on Wednesday to ENCORE office, and on Thursday to a grass roots project at the south end of the Island to view a project similar in process to one we might set up (or attempt to) on Dominica. ENCORE stands for Environmental and Coastal Resources, and as I may have mentioned before, will be the Agency/Project overseeing myself and the other three environmental types on Dominica.

But more on that after I get to Dominica. For now I've discovered a good portion of our training takes place outside of class. So what else is new! This weekend saw me dissolved in tears, sitting on the back steps of my home stay's house. The reason, you ask? I cooked for the first time! Actually, as all of you who cry easily understand, many events lead up to the actual burst, and Sunday morning was no exception.

I'd known a week ago that I was going to prepare the Sunday meal. I'd also known that my home stay father, Julian, would take me shopping. Julian does the shopping for the family. He has a small van provided to him by the company he works for, Care Service, a pest control firm; otherwise his wife would have to ride the transport from Babonneau, seven miles to Castries, shop and return home via transport carrying her packages, then walk one mile to home!

Things: food, clothing, articles are all expensive here! So, I worried about what to buy, what to cook, how to prepare it, the cost, would it taste good, would my home stay family like it, how long would it take to prepare, would I get home and have the right ingredients! Between all this worrying (which I do so well), a group of Volunteers scheduled a party which I couldn't go to because that was when Julian was taking me shopping; it was Friday before I finally decided what to cook and made a list and found a cookbook; Friday we also got typhoid shots that were supposed to make us ILL! And I was homesick! Not bad my first day since I left Auburn.

Can you just imagine what I learned from that "hands-on" experience? I learned shopping is easy if you go with a local, but don't go on Friday afternoon. I learned how hot a small kitchen gets when you bake banana bread for 1 ½ hours! I learned how much propane it takes to cook rice, stir fry and bake banana bread. I learned next time I'll cook the meat ahead of time till TENDER, and then add it to my vegetables; I'll cook the rice way ahead of time; in fact, I may never cook stir fry for two years!

The rice took 1 ½ hours to cook because my young home stay sister Hermia put in way too much water! Which was really to my advantage because then the meat cooked longer! I forgot to mention I marinated cucumbers, tomatoes and onion in oil and vinegar and sugar which also turned out okay because the family put this concoction on the stir fry (actually a well-cooked dish) and thoroughly enjoyed the combination. They are the most polite people I have ever met! The banana nut bread (raisins instead of nuts) was delicious, and Madeleine (home stay mom) wants to make it again with grated coconut added.

I've forgotten to mention the real contributing factor which burst the dam. Early that morning Madeleine had mentioned that she wanted to leave on our trip to the beach and to the north part of the Island at 1:00 p.m.! Now, here again, the personality culture, upbringing, past experiences of this particular Peace Corps trainee come into play! Be honest now in assessing this event. Have you ever known me to be late!

You must also add to this assessment a very hot kitchen, three hours standing on my feet making banana bread and chopping meat and vegetables; the radio preaching to me about my sins and how I can stay out of hell; a fourteen-year-old daughter helping me all she can; and the clock continuing to tick away; 12:00, 12:30, 1:00, 1:30, 2:00 – we eat at 2:30, leave the dishes and are on the road at 3:30!

I didn't actually start crying until 12:30. And, of course, I told them it was because I was making them late for the outing! Do you know what they did? Laughed and laughed and laughed! Madelaine said, "If we tell Julian he will roll on the floor!" Hermia fixed me a glass of orange juice. Julian picked flowers and put them on my chest of drawers in the bedroom. And I learned an incredible lesson on what's known as St. Lucian time!

Their sense of humor, insight and understanding was so incredible! The outing included my first swim in the Caribbean at a spot called Pidgeon Point – white sand and all! They call it bathing – can

I ever float in the salt water. After our "bath" we drove around the local "subdivision." One particular one called CAP Estates was on high hills overlooking the sea. Definitely how the other half lives – sprawling houses, expansive gardens and VIEWS! If the day had been less hazy we could have seen the island of Martinique, 120 miles away I kept remembering all the drives I'd taken in all my years looking at houses! Couples are the same the world over!

Other weekend happenings included a walk through the back property to see gardens (vegetable) and trees. No cars, just peace and quiet. We saw a white heron standing right next to a tethered cow, an iridescent hummingbird just in front of us. The hummingbird had a small diamond-shaped shield on its head placed something like the top-knot of a Steller's jay! This diamond flashed silver and turquoise in the sun. During lunch yesterday, a brilliant yellow canary lit in the coconut tree outside the dining room window. On Saturday night we took a drive to the next community. The roads were a conglomeration of pickups, vans, cars, people walking and visiting – some dressed in their Saturday night finery, a wedding reception and a disco also spilling out onto the local streets. Julian took me by his adopted father's house. It was about 9:30 at night and they were working in a carpentry shop building a decorative form for their church building. Before that I'd helped a young man put together a jigsaw puzzle in a home at a spot called Paix Bouche (Pay Boosh) where we could see the lights of Castries below.

We've been given the words to Dominica's national song. Beautiful! The first four lines of the first verse are:

Isle of beauty, Isle of splendor,
Isle to all so sweet and fair.
All must surely gaze in wonder
At thy gifts so rich and rare!

We've also learned that the Eastern Caribbean is known as the "Land of the three Ses." Sun, sea and sex! Saw a frigate bird catch a fish in the surf at Pidgeon Point. The weather people have predicted a wave, which means a low pressure area which can produce a storm, something we've not had since I arrived. My homestay family say a wave can bring high winds and lots and lots of rain – maybe two or three days of heavy rain. They say you usually stay in during a bad storm! So far we have had at least one, maybe more, showers each day I've been here.

One day, on a trip into Castries and the bank and post office, I got rained on and completely dried out three times! And I love the sound of the rain at night on the roof and front porch. My room is in the middle of the house with a window opening to the front porch or veranda. It is a cozy place and I do lots of writing and reading sitting up in bed.

I've learned from the Peace Corps sessions that we may not write anything for any type of publication without having our material cleared by the Peace Corps. So, if any of you have a newsletter that you thought about putting my letter in, please don't do that. The problem seems to be a sensitivity to local feelings. I might write something that is perceived differently by someone who lives here.

I'm looking forward to hearing from you. I heard from Kathryn Beggs who also sent excerpts from the Sentinel. Thank you!

Take care!
Love, Mary Ann

August 1, 1992 – St Lucia

Dear Family and Friends:

If it can be said that the experience gets better each day, then today was the best! Many, many things contributed to its being good, just like so many things led up to last Sunday's outburst of tears.

Yesterday Friday, was the last day all of the volunteers/trainees were together for training. On Tuesday, four people leave for St. Vincent, the St. Lucia trainees begin their work assignments and all the education people start their practice teaching The rest of us technical types will focus on individual projects, agency visits, and 1 ½ hours of daily language training (both French and English Creole).

I'll (hopefully) learn French Creole. To hear it spoken (not by me) is such an experience. It has feeling, emotion, accents, and a range of vocal sounds! At this point, I haven't the foggiest idea what is being said. But I sure like to listen.

The French and English Creole spoken in the Eastern Caribbean originated out of the need of the African slaves to communicate with one another and their English or French masters. When the slaves were brought to the Islands and sold to the plantation owners, they were usually separated from all the rest of their family and friends so they could not talk and conspire against the master. Because the slaves came from many, many different African tribes, all speaking different dialects, more often than not the slaves found themselves working and living with people they could not talk to!

I've learned a few words:

Bonjou – good morning
Bonse – good evening
Bonn apwe hidi – good afternoon
Sa ka fet? Kouman ou ye? – How are you?

The people also greet one another at nighttime by saying, "Good night." At first I thought they were just leaving when they had just arrived. Now that official language classes have begun I should improve. Some of the young trainees are already speaking phrases!

After Friday's final get-together some of us went to a Babonneau community barbeque. It was held on the school grounds in front of Babonneau Catholic Church: barbequed chicken, (fig) banana salad, coleslaw, bak (a fried bread), beer, soft drinks and juice. Alcohol on school grounds is still permissible here. The music (by popular Hi-Fi) was LOUD! Much twisting and turning, moving about and foot tapping went on, but no real dancing. One style done in the discos is called "belt polishing."

Mary Petersen, P.C. trainee from Missouri, and I got a ride in the back of a pickup truck to the barbeque. I walked home by flashlight with two other trainees who live just across from me. Women who walk alone at night are considered available and, for a P.C. person, open to assault.

The barbeque was my first community experience except for church services. Watching the young men and women vie for attention or being ignored or doing the ignoring is fascinating. Both sexes can really look charming! There are always many more men than women out and about. The women are masters at ignoring or tossing remarks back!

Friday noon I'd gone downtown from school on the transport to purchase something for a big Saturday Peace Corps picnic. In the middle of Castries, teeming with people, I met three local people that I knew. They took me in the tow and showed me the marketplace, a bakery, a photo shop and a farm supply store associated with the Ministry of Agriculture. (I'll discuss the market someday.)

Mina, who took me around, lives just beside my homestay's driveway and I stop and visit (chat outside) each evening on my way home. She gardens and sells her goods, mostly herbs and celery, at the open street market in Castries. She is at the market some days by 5:30 a.m. to get a good location.

That day Mina had taken a sprinkler head with her to buy a new one. But the farm supply was out of that style for the next two weeks! She was disappointed! When I stop each evening, she always gives me something. A few nights ago it was a coconut that had firm meat inside instead of jelly. The jelly coconuts are the little children's favorite!

First, the hard outside shell is chopped partway off with a long-handled blade that I call a cutlass. Then a swift chop of the blade opens up a hole just large enough to drink coconut water from by lifting the whole coconut, when the water has gone, the coconut is chopped in two, again with one swift knife movement. A small piece of outer shell is sliced off with a third swift motion and the coconut and scoop are ready for someone to scoop out soft coconut jelly. I like the water and really love the firm coconut meat, but I'll leave the jelly for the young ones!

Mina explained to me that most St. Lucian men want two, three or four women or wives. But, she said, in her case she was not about to allow this! I like Mina. She has lots of spunk and works so hard keeping her garden in order. Her herbs seem to be in demand. Her husband is a taxi driver and on Sunday (his day off), he arises at 5:30 a.m. and turns the radio on FULL blast to a country western station. All the neighbors wish he wouldn't but one tells him so!

August 2, 1992 - St Lucia – Sunday

I've gotten a long way from telling you why yesterday was so good! So back on track.

Friday night's barbeque was the first evening I'd been away from the family. I think they were feeling the strain as much as I! Then Saturday morning Hermia, Jervan, Madaliene and I went to a wedding in Marchand – just outside of Castries. It was a Catholic wedding in one of the large Catholic churches. All are huge and beautiful in their simplicity. They are all constructed basically alike; a long, wide, tall center section separated by large pillars and arches from two outer sections of equal length but of lesser ceiling height and narrower width. The outer walls are a combination of eight feet of solid wall and eight feet of open space. The windows, so typical of large buildings here, especially the schools, are row after row of square nine inch openings. The window sections are placed opposite each other on the outer walls and create this marvelous breeze inside the buildings. Well, it is marvelous if the breeze is already blowing outside. The inside of the churches are painted in soft greens or yellows. Oftentimes the center arched ceiling is made of inlaid wood, other times, tin.

Saturday's wedding was quite small compared to a few the other trainees have attended, but I loved it. The bride was late. Bands play in the churches here. During the wedding, the response (a traditional part of the ceremony) was done via a saxophone solo! Nice!) The ring bearer and flower girl were so precious I couldn't hold back the tears! The little boy and girl were all dressed in white outfits pressed to perfection, their black hair, eyes and faces contrasting brilliantly. The wedding began at 8:30 and was finished (including the baptism of a baby) by 10:00 a.m.

My homestay family went to church after the wedding. I got to come home all by myself!!! I got ready for the picnic and while waiting for my ride I called Lori in Auburn. I told her how nice it was to be alone! Can you imagine, it was the first time I'd been by myself since I'd left Auburn on July 11th. Now that may not sound like a big deal to many of you, but after 14 years of single life. On the phone I got to listen to Kyle say, "Hi, Grandma" before he ran off. Lori and I were having a nice conversation when the rain began. I should say rain and wind. Before I could get all the windows closed, the dining room table, chairs and floor were puddles! So instead of spending more time on the phone with Lori, I had to hang up and mop the floor! Who said this was any different than home?

Today, Sunday, I washed! This involves filling a large plastic tub with soap and water and clothes in the shower (only cold water in this house). Next I sit on the shower stall short wall – it is about five inches high – with the tub between my feet and knees and scrub away! Madaliene says the clothes are not coming clean unless you make this squeaking sound between your palm, clothes and wrist. She has such a motion and makes such a squish! But then she helped raise a few brothers and sisters and the washing was done in the river. Madaliene says washing is relaxing! She just listens to the swish and feels the soap suds.

Friday we also lost our fourth trainee. I didn't hear details, but I think this young lady returned to the States for a boyfriend, also. None of the older volunteers have called it quits yet, although one lady has very swollen ankles, legs and knees. Last weekend two volunteers were riding in the back of a pickup with their homestay family. The driver was going too fast and crashed into a brick wall. I think it happened about midnight and all was very scary. One gal lost a tooth and the other lady is very bruised up. They are both going to stay, but the "powers that be" say they'll probably write a policy about riding in the back of pickup trucks. I guess there is no speed limit! The vehicle problem is a whole other story! Supposedly, in Dominica they can put every person who lives there in the cars on that island!

Yesterday, my homestay family couldn't go to the picnic because they are Seventh Day Adventists. But I think everyone else went. Good. Good. Good! Finally, the Caribbean like it's supposed to be:

sun, sand, surf, palm trees, off-shore islands, and a bay with sailboats, food and friends. We even had a troupe of dancers come and entertain us! Add to the above all the food we could eat, drinks, a pickup load of coconuts, children covering themselves with sand, playing volleyball, swimmers, snorkelers and Calypso music!

That morning had been my first alone experience – that day was my first truly relaxing experience! I swam, ate, talked, listened, watched, took photos, and best of all lay on the lovely white Caribbean sand.

Among all these events and scenes are sprinkled day to day Caribbean living, like how to get someplace on time and what is "on time," what kind of transportation should be taken and does it work; and what should be worn. I know why P.C. trainees aren't given more to do – adjusting is a full-time job!

I keep saying I'm not writing so many letters, but then these experiences keep happening and I get excited. Today we drove on a ridge in the middle of the island. We could see the Caribbean and Martinique out the left window and the Atlantic outside the right window. St. Lucia is 14 miles across at its widest point; Martinique a mere 20-some miles away.

I miss home and all of you! But this is such a good thing, too! Love, Mary Ann

August 11, 1992 – St Lucia

Dear Mom and Bill:

I got your letter and note. Thank you so much. I guess it's hard to imagine how much the mail means to me. All of my letters, your letters, have lifted my spirits each time one has arrived. Mom, your news of all is welcome and I'm glad you enjoy my letters. I love writing them and knowing people are interested.

Bill, I wish you were here taking my language lessons! They (the language lessons) are hard for me. It is not really a written language, only passed on orally. The two fellows in charge of our lessons are writing it down and we do have the benefit of their expertise. Also, I understand when we got to Dominica (pronounced Dominik in Creole) we will have tapes and curriculum. So things may look up. Then again

I've heard from a number of people, thanks to your efforts. Sure do appreciate that!

August 11, 1992; St Lucia 12:30 p.m. Tuesday

Bonn apwemidi Family and Friends:

Translated your greeting means: "Good afternoon." It is pronounced Bo apwaymede. Learning French Creole is not easy for me! It is such a challenge and continually on my mind! Tomorrow we go to market and order/buy food, fruits and vegetables – using Creole. I'd better shape up or I'm liable to starve on Dominica.

Just in case you are interested, "Mwen ka ale Donmic eve twavayan ofisye enviwon" means "I am going to Dominica and working as an environmental official or an official of the environment."

Sounds pretty official! But I still don't know what to expect – a pretty usual happening in the Eastern Caribbean Peace Corps.

Next week at this time I'll be on Dominica! I can hardly wait! Rumor has it that a young lady named Melanie from Virginia and I will be placed in Portsmouth. The other two environmental types will be in Scotts Head. But that may and can change at any moment.

We fly out of Castries Vegie Airport on Monday, August 17, and stay with Roseau, Dominica homestays for six days and then are on our own! We get sworn in by Dominican Prime Minister Eugena Charles on Wednesday!

You may write (until a new address emerges) to:

PCV – Mary Ann Kollenberg
PC Dominica
P.O. Box 357
Roseau, Dominica W.I.

Speaking of writing. Your letters have been the most exciting thing to happen every time they arrive, which may mean I'm having a hard time letting go! But you'll have to admit you are some pretty special people to let go of! Did I tell you Kayla's crawling? Lori says she needs watching every single minute! She never stops! Kyle takes little sister Kayla my postcards and tells her, "This is from Grandma. She's still in the middle of the ocean."

Speaking of grandchildren, the next time you see Josh ask to see the photos I sent him. This past Sunday I visited the neighbors at the top of the lane where I live. Their name is Popo. A mom, dad, two sons and a daughter live in a small house just next to the road. My homestay mom, Madaleine, had gotten permission for me to hang my clothes on their line; so when I was taking the clothes down, Ethaliene, the mom, and I talked. Her son Lucius, 23, turned out to be the "Commonwealth Champion in Black Belt Karate," and "National Karate (Person) of the Year." His trophies line three shelves! They showed me stacks of photos and Lucius generously gave me three photos for Josh, two he autographed!

As you can gather, Sunday also saw me washing again. This time I washed Sunday morning and had my clothes hung out to dry by 10:00 a.m. then taken in and ironed by 3:00 p.m. I must say, the sweat can really roll over a hot iron on an Eastern Caribbean afternoon! I've got to find a way to get clothes that require less ironing! If you've any light cotton/polyester, size 10-12, lying around that you're not using, please send! (my colors are pink, blue, rose, greens, lilacs!) Also, it seems to be a lot like camping/hiking – especially with Markley's group – I'm not aware of body odor at least not my own!

I need to catch you up on all the happenings since my last letter – no easy task considering the events taking place and the fact each meal is an experience in itself, not to mention all the other things like a trip around the island, the mangrove sanctuary, sea moss farmers, and love making in the tour plane!

You all know how I am about stories – I love them. Well, almost everything here involves a story, so most of the time I'm pretty content. Not happy yet; it seems I still have lots of crying to do – but this too shall pass! Also, yesterday and today, the aches and pains surfaced worse than they ever had in California. Yesterday turned into a six-aspirin day! But I've got it figured out! It's called a low pressure system coupled with wrestling a 19-month-old live-wire, walking five miles on an Eastern Caribbean afternoon on pavement, eating all these starches and stressing out over Creole.

Not only that, Madaleine has been complaining of bursitis pains that don't go away in the morning after a good night's sleep. So I looked through the good 'ole Peace Corps medical kit and sure enough found some mild pain relievers for minor pain. I've heard it before. I suggested she try one, and I've yet to see the bottle again. Lesson number 99 learned by experience. I'm sure that's why language training is so difficult. I'm such an experiential learner.

Would you like to go around the island first or hear about the tour plane? Chronologically the island came first, but the tour plane trip was really great.

Have I mentioned before about the four Dominica environmental people – trip to Vieux Fort at the south of the island to visit CANARIES (Caribbean Natural Resources Institute)? Well, last Thursday we visited the CANARIS' field projects; sea moss farming, charcoal making from the mangrove trees, and plantation plantings of alternative species for making charcoal. (I tried my darndest to say that last one in simpler terms!)

Our field guide for the CANARIES was Mathias Burt, a pleasant, intelligent, congenial St. Lucian with a good sense of humor. He showed us the mangrove sanctuary, about 100 acres of red, black and white mangrove trees, where local people make charcoal. As you know, the mangrove is saline tolerant with the red mangrove growing at the fringes where the salt concentration is highest and the black and white mangrove growing further inland. I continually marvel at the adaptability of plants and in this case wonder how long it took the mangrove to evolve.

The red mangrove was the most fascinating with its long shoots or suckers growing downward from the branches until they reached the soggy soil where they began to sprout up again. Each branch also had long narrow pods that when they dry (still attached to their mother branch) act like a "Scud missile" and shoot straight down into the soil or water, depending on tide and rainy season, to solidly anchor themselves and begin a new plant! The mangrove leaves sparkled in the sunlight with salt crystals that had worked their way from the salt water taken in at the roots to the leaves. A button wood is also associated with the mangrove forest, as is in this case, a clinging, choking parasitic plant called the love vine! Not at all my idea of love!

During World War II the USA used this very same mangrove forest to camouflage their planes. They cut a road right through the middle of the forest – it is still there and is the same one we traveled on. Then off of this main road they cut smaller openings into the forest. These smaller openings were used to hide their airplanes, covered by the dense branches of the mangrove trees.

Today the small road and narrow openings are called tour planes, and according to our guide, are the site of many accidents because they are perfect spots for love making and many accidents occur as one set of lovers drives in just as a second set is leaving!

Now that experience – seeing the mangroves – would have been ample, but what happened net has got to be my St. Lucian highlight! We drove through the mangrove forest to the edge of the

Atlantic Ocean, hence along a dirt road lined with coconut palms for about a mile. The Caribbean is lovely, but that day the Atlantic on St. Lucia's eastern shore sparkled turquoise green and azure blue and lapped on the white sand beach as if to say, "I Welcome You!" It was the first time I'd touched the Atlantic Ocean. We ate our lunch in the van and then raised our skirts, rolled up our pants, whichever was appropriate took off our shoes and nonchalantly, without a care in the world, walked for about a mile on the beach to the sea moss farm. Absolutely the only thing I did wrong that day was to leave my camera at home! I've already taken over 100 slides!

The sea moss, a type of seaweed, is grown commercially on ropes strung from pole to pole or stake to stake just offshore and kept afloat with plastic bottles. Each line is from 30-50 feet long and the seed moss is attached to the rope by "twining" it through the loops as the rope is "pulled open." It costs about $20 EC for a rope and sea moss – the bottles can be picked up anywhere – and in about four to six weeks a farmer can harvest his first crop and raise about $100 EC or reinvest it on additional ropes.

Space in the sea is leased from the Department of Fisheries. On the Island of St. Lucia, the beach is free to the public except at one spot in the north part of the island. The public can walk, bathe, swim, picnic on any beach up to 197 meters above the high tide mark. It is a marvelous thing!

At the sea moss farm, two fun things happened. Mathias found a coconut and cracked it by simply hitting it against a tree. He held it up, opened his mouth and let all the coconut water run in his mouth and down his chin. When the water was gone he raised his head and laughingly apologized for being so greedy, but then took a cutlass and cut the coconut into pieces for us to relish! At another point during our trip, Mathias climbed a mango tree and got each of us a mango – which we greedily and messily devoured.

The second fun thing at the sea moss farm was meeting a farmer who was camping on the beach for four days while he tended his sea moss. "Short Man," as he was called (he was under five feet tall) explained the whole proce. from the initial twining of the seed moss to the harvesting of the mature plant. There was not one among us who wasn't about ready to retire and become a sea moss farmer. Just as a side note, this project was helped along by CANARIES, but initiated by the fishermen themselves. It is better quality sea moss, keep the natural growing sea moss from being depleted, gathers good organisms to the beds for feed, and is evidently leading to an increase in lobsters because baby lobsters are finding it a popular, healthy place to hang out! In addition to all of that, the farmers cannot satisfy the market, and one of the island's main hotels is working on a sea moss drink! For those of you who don't know – I didn't – sea moss is used in jellies, gelatin, some perfumes, et cetera.

All of that and I forgot to explain the process of making charcoal. But you've probably seen that on Channel 6. We met three of the charcoal makers, one very elderly and two young. This is definitely a craft that must be learned by doing. Vocational education is alive and well on this island – not necessarily in the classroom, but surely in the field.

Speaking of "up there in age," I met a lady on the transport yesterday who proudly told me she was 82. In fact, she said, "I still do my own shopping and can thread a needle without glasses!" She hopped off the transport like a woman half her age, groceries and all!

If you can read anymore, I'll tell you about our holiday trip around the island. It seems the first Monday of every month is a holiday – so we planned a picnic and trip for Sunday, August 3rd, and we're going to rest on the 4th. My homestays are Seventh Day Adventists so this meant in order to leave early on the 3rd, we had to prepare the picnic food after sundown on Saturday. The Sabbath begins on Friday at sundown and ends on Saturday at sundown. During Sabbath this family does not work, not even dishes. All the food is prepared Friday and only reheated on Saturday!

So on Saturday after sundown the dishes had to be done and picnic prepared! We did it! Saturday night and Sunday morning it poured and kept pouring, so we didn't go on our trip and ate the picnic lunch around the dining room table.

I should mention a picnic is simply foods you would cook at home to eat a normal meal: meat, potatoes, rice, salad, beans and taken with you. All the glasses and plates are household items – all is packed in a box. Only juice is treated differently in that ice is carried separately, wrapped in an insulated container.

Because the preparation is so involved, we decided to postpone the trip until the 9th – but then it cleared Sunday afternoon and we decided if the weather held we'd tour the island the next day. But heaven forbid we should prepare another picnic. So I suggested I'd treat them to lunch if a reasonable spot could be found. Monday dawned beautifully. Here that means blue sky and fast moving white clouds accompanied by soft winds and a myriad of sounds!

Now no one bothered to tell me, other than we couldn't see too much, why it was a good reason to stay home on a rainy day. At least on the road to Soufriere. It seems the St. Lucian government is improving the road from Castries to Canaries (pronounce canneries). It has been finished only partway to a spot called Roseau Valley. As most of you know, I've been on a few four-wheel drive roads, but this road from Roseau Valley to Canaries equaled the best!

Roseau Valley was the site of St. Lucia's largest sugar cane plantation during the slavery era. One of the many horrible things done to keep the slaves from running into the hills, involved the importing of poisonous snakes! Evidently, when they were grading the road on the high ridges above Roseau Valley, snakes by the bucketsful were uncovered. One report said the workers hung the dead snakes in trees alongside the road! The original sugar cane fields is still on the valley floor and the land now a large banana (fig in Creole) plantation! It is hard for me to look into the eyes of the West Indian males and not see the sadness of their ancestors who worked in the fields.

Our main destination for the day's outing was actually a town called Soufriere. It's been nominated as a world-class historical monument. Many of its French architectural building still stand and we saw a solidly-built canal still transporting water that was building 1765.

In Canaries we passed across the Canaries River, its river rock covered with drying clothes and women still washing in the stream. Upstream we saw a bright red pickup truck parked squarely in the middle of the river the driver scrubbing away on the pickup.

One we crawled our way through the roadwork and arrived on just the old road to Soufriere, it was like driving in a green wonderland. Mountains on one side, Caribbean on the other, giant ferns, in green, green, green! The road was narrow under a lush canopy and wound around curve after curve until it climbed the mountain then descended into the Valley of Soufriere.

Such a vista at our first overlook! Far below us was this valley ending at the blue-green sea. At the valley floor, a small colorful village all set against a backdrop of St. Lucia's Petit Piton! You'll have to see the slides!

St. Lucia's two Pitons – Petit Piton and Gros Piton. The smaller one seems the bigger because it is always seen at a closer distance. Beside these two volcanic cones, the Soufriere area, features botanical gardens, mineral baths, the beautiful Diamond Waterfall, and a drive through volcano with sulfur springs. The center of the volcano collapsed forming a caldera which is full of bubbling, hot, sizzling steam and gas rising up out of numerous mounded vents. The more it rains, the higher the steam rises. We got there just following a downpour.

Don't I sound just like a tour guide? Our day around the island went well, and we found a nice restaurant that I could afford. That's not always the case, you know.

I've heard from a number of you who receive this bit of news from the Eastern Caribbean. I'm glad you are enjoying my letters. You know I love to write them, and it is such a marvelous feeling to know you are sharing my experience. Until next time, Bonswe (Goodnight).

Fondly, Mary Ann

P.S. Forgive me if I get carried away now. I'm sure I won't be able to keep this up for two years.

August 17, 1992; 9:30 a.m.; St. Lucia, West Indies

Dear Family and Friends:

I am packed and waiting for the van to take me to the Vegie Airport for the flight to Dominica. The local joke about the name of this flight, "LIAT" is that it stands for "Leave the Island Anytime!" So, I have a feeling that the 12:55 scheduled flight may leave anytime but 12:55!

I'm actually quite sad about leaving Babonneau. The folks here, including my own homestay family, have been so gracious. Last night the homestays in Paix Bouche (Pay Boosh), just up the road from Babonneau, gave all of us a going-away party; food, drinks, music and all. Yesterday for lunch, Madaleine and Julian took me to The Lime, a local but touristy place at Rodney Bay. It was fun dining out, but poor Madaleine got a tummy ache! She is deathly afraid of lizards and one lovely blue and orange fellow kept checking on our table. Then Jervan kept up his normal behavior which increased her stress level. This brought back memories of eating out with the youngsters. We never had lizards, though!

Following lunch we toured the Windjammer Resort, one of the Island's newest fancy places. Not to worry about staying there – its $180 U.S. per night, off season, for a one-bedroom villa. And only $500 U.S. per night during the season for a three-bedroom villa with private pool. Above prices do not include meals, et cetera, et cetera, et cetera!

After I finished packing today I sat on the back steps at "home" and ate a mango. I've developed a taste for them. Yesterday, I drank the water from two coconuts, each in less than five minutes. For breakfast I had a banana, an orange, sweet potato pudding and an egg with lettuce on wheat bread. The biggest treat here seems to be cocoa tea. Yummy! It is grated cocoa mixed with boiling water, sugar and a little cinnamon then strained and served in a mug with hot milk!

August 17, 1992 - 5:30 p.m. Dominica

Dear Folks:

I'm in Roseau, Dominica! Sitting on a second-story veranda overlooking busy Cork Street, wires going everywhere, poles, tin roofs of every color (green, orange, red, rusty brown), peaked roofs with gable ends, hipped roofs with dormers. Opposite is a bakery at street level with a restaurant above, also with a full balcony, plants hanging everywhere! Diagonally across from the restaurant is the house of the President of Dominica, Sir Clarence Signoret. No state house for him, according to my hostess, Ruth Nicolos, he is a very common man and prefers to live in his old family home in the middle of downtown Roseau.

Ruth, my Roseau homestay mom for this week, is a lovely 72-year-old retired lady who never married. She says she is "single, free and happy." She was a bank clerk at Barclay's Bank in Roseau for 37 years. Actually, she retired in 1976, but they hired her back for ten years as Public Relations Manager (four hours a day). She officially retired in 1986. The bank gave her three months' vacation every three years when she'd travel to London or the States!

On Cork Street standing under the restaurant balcony is a policeman. Ruth tells me she has no thieves – no wonder!

I am so happy to be here! We flew from St. Lucia in a small 19-seater, and had been warned of the landing at Canefield Airport. But not even a bump on landing! The flight took one hour and most of the hour seemed taken up by flying along the Martinique coast. After St. Lucia, Martinique looked gigantic. In one of my letters I mentioned Martinique was 120 miles from St. Lucia. Sorry. It's only 40.

I believe Dominica gets something like 386 inches of rain a year. We've already been greeted in Dominica fashion! Rain and more rain. Dominica is so different than St. Lucia. Somehow neater. Much, much less populated. The mountains rise straight up in the center of the Island, starting almost at the coast. I felt welcomed, at home, the minute we landed.

Marie Hitchman, PCV from Bellingham, Washington, is staying in Ruth's house, too. It will be fun to have a "roomy" for a while, especially one my own age. Some of us "older" types continue to have identity crises from being around the young people so much. Their priorities are so different than ours. In fact, I'm sending home a newsletter written during training. And, don't get me wrong, but most of the experiences in the newsletter were not mine! And that was perfectly okay! I'm also enclosing, with this letter, a copy of a poem written by a young black woman for a PCV after the volunteer used words like dark, gloomy, witches, death and dying to describe the word BLACK to her students in an exercise about color. You be the judge!

The street below my veranda is like the ones I described in Castries with each building opening onto the sidewalk. It is dusk and the sky a soft blue; slow grey-white clouds passing by. The street noises have subsided. I wish the cars could mysteriously disappear.

In church on Saturday in Babonneau I spoke to the congregation and thanked them for making us feel so welcome. It was special for them and for me. And best of all, I got to publicly thank Madaleine and Julian. They just beamed! Darkness is fast falling. I'll continue in the morning.

August 18, 1992 6:30 a.m.

Woke up this a.m. to the sound of vehicles on the narrow street below, a lady sweeping and washing the street in front of the bakery. Cork Street was not closed to traffic during the night! Need I say more? I think about 11:30 I resorted to earplugs. So much for the romantic veranda room above a charming street!

Before I left St. Lucia I got a haircut, shampoo and blow-dry in a lovely West Indian salon. The shop looked out over, what else? the Caribbean! Only a few minor problems – each item cost a different amount: haircut $15.00 EC, shampoo and blow-dry $25 EC! So after $40.00 I was clipped, shampooed and dried, a little more than I'd intended! Lesson learned – always ask first!

Last Thursday morning during language class – I still struggle and struggle – we were told about a special program at the Central Library in Castries put on by the St. Lucian Folk Research Center. My heavens, did it turn out to be special! The focus of this program was keeping Creole alive. There were speakers, video tapes, films and live performers. An older West Indian gentleman spoke on the move to preserve the language, one, as I've mentioned before, that has evolved orally. One video highlighted a small village, Paya, whose descendants came from Africa after the slave movement and the research being done on this mini-culture. The villagers are also adept at an African dance they are keeping alive! The older women and men are the best dancers. They teach the young.

The two live performances focused on the outside influences that have hindered Creole: An educational system that stresses English, T.V., and pressures of society to speak English, to name a few. The live performances were done by amateurs from all over the Island. Imagine my surprise at realizing I knew one of the fellows wielding a cutlass in the small semi-circle in front of me. It was none other than Mathias Burt, our guide from the mangrove and sea moss projects. I felt, once again, like I was part of the Eastern Caribbean experience – drums, drama, colorful clothes, dramatic sounds, black faces and accented voices. They acted, danced, spoke and moved – all to the rhythm of their drums and music of the Creole language.

August 21, 1992; 3:30 p.m. Friday

It's been a few days since I finished the paragraphs above. So much has happened. One thing I'll say for Peace Corps, they keep you busy. Yesterday was the first day of house hunting, and reality has set in! Before that we were involved in the transition from Peace Corps trainees to full-fledged Peace Corps volunteers, a visit with the President of Dominica, our swearing in, and getting to know the continuing Island volunteers and Peace Corps staff. The continual adjusting and what it does to the emotions, physical well-being, and hence to the energy level in this heat is amazing. All of the "old" volunteers (ones who've been here a year) have hollow eyes! That's scary.

It is hot! And has been since our second day on Dominica. We've had a storm scare, but no one here really panics – but do they ever listen to the news! We received our hurricane training via handouts, personal discussions and a video of a real-live hurricane. M homestay mom, Ruth, says lots of praying goes on in this house. So we are safe! During Hurricane David in 1979 her house (and more important, her roof) stood! She gives all the credit to God hearing her praying.

I've been placed in Portsmouth at the north of the Island for my two-year stint. Portsmouth is about one hour from Roseau and is known as the "second town." All other spots on the Island are called communities or villages. Melanie, who is also going to Portsmouth, and I traveled there yesterday to look for housing. We found a few spots; two flats, fairly new, with a bathroom, kitchen and bedroom. These rooms were in Portsmouth. We also located a three-bedroom home on an estate (plantation) about a mile outside of town. Transportation, water and the landlady all make the three-bedroom spot undesirable. But oh, what a location! The water system is by cistern but the pump was recently stolen. The landlady has a poor reputation with previous PC renters.

The reality of Portsmouth may take some adjustment on my part. All I have to say at this point is, "There is lots to do." One young man, after being given his assignment, said," "Remember, we're here to go where they need us, not to go where we want to go!"

Tomorrow we are off for a day of swimming in the Layou River. Dominican rivers, most of them, are all beautiful, wide and rushing!

The automobile is a double-edged sword. Just like St. Lucia, life is made easier, foods get to market faster, and many Dominicans are more independent. But, oh, the noise and congestion on their narrow, pedestrian crowded streets becomes a daily nightmare.

Marie and I walked to the Botanical Gardens today. Nice! They were begun in 1890. So many trees are huge – especially a banyan tree – probably the only one in the whole garden I recognized. My favorite sight was the wild forested ridge rising just east of the garden's boundary. When we finally get to visit the rain forest I just know I'll love it! My friend from Missouri, Mary Peterson, whom I've mentioned before, has been assigned to teach on the Carib Reserve. She is just thrilled! Here on the Island, we older types outnumber the younger ones and everyone seems far more serious. Actually, not serious but more mature. It is good to be in the majority for a while.

And speaking of maturity, the powers that be selected Portsmouth for my site because they felt I would add stability to the area. Seems there are a number of problems; drugs, the opposition party is in the majority, many factions want their own projects moved forward, economics and unemployment. I believe I'm going to resort to Ruth's hurricane remedy.

It continues to amaze me that so much living on the Islands is focused inward. Here is such beauty all around, but seldom enjoyed. Maybe that is a truism world-wide!

I think my writing is running out for today – so until next time – love and miss you all. Your letters all are so, so welcomed.

Love, Mary Ann.
P.S. We left Vegie Airport on time! The National Geographic June 1990 edition has a great article on Dominica.

> What is Black?
> Black is the shine of ebony
> And the colour of some people's hair
> Black is the feather of the Corbeau king

And the skin of my ancestors

Black is the seed of the sweet Sapo dita

Black is the forerunner of the fair dawn

Black is Truth

Black is Justice

Black is Beautiful

Black is the writing of Martin Luther King

And the words of Malcolm X

Black is the philosophy of Marcus Garvey

And the teaching of Bustamonte

Black is the roll of the Tumba drums

And the dancing of the Shango women

Black is the taste of molasses sweet

And the culture of my people

Black is the son of King Shaka

And the daughter of Queen Nazinga

Black is the ring of the short-knees gullo

Black is Free

Black is We

Black is being Me

August 21, 1992

Dear Mom and Bill:

It is unbearably hot! Usually at this time of day I'm either in a vehicle or at the Peace Corps office (there are ceiling fans there). Today I'm at my Roseau, Dominica, homestay's house, in my room on the second floor! I have a portable fan placed on a chair blowing on me. But, oh it is still hot!

I'm in possession of three notes from you – the latest received today, was forwarded from St. Lucia. You postmarked it on August 5th! It contained all the family news which I loved. Thank you. Glad to hear Craig came down, that Billie and M celebrated their 50th, that John's play is another success. I had been in on painting job after the fact, too. I was visiting Uncle Johnny on the day the painter came back to take a photo of his work.

The other two notes you wrote arrived in Dominica, one preceded me! So it was here when I arrived. This bit of news here on this page is the first time I've written, even in my journal, since receiving that note. But I think I've recovered my desire to correspond again. Thank you for sending the second note so promptly. It helped put the wind back in my sails. It seems I rely a great deal on sharing my experiences with my friends as well as my family.

I'm sure I won't keep up this pace for the full two years, letter writing pace that is. And you did make me realize I could be more selective in what I wrote. The only problem with that being I'll have to edit and rewrite everything, something I can't find time or energy to do. Hopefully that will change, too.

I've written Lori and asked her to give you money for the copying. Accu-Copy on Borland is fairly reasonable. I realize what a task that all is. I appreciate it, and from your second note, so do others. Thank you, too, for sending the typewritten copies. It will help the memory and also help me to see where I need to improve my letter writing.

The first part of the enclosed general letter was written just prior to leaving St. Lucia and just after arriving in Dominica. You'll note, as I continue writing, a little of the excitement of Dominica has worn off. Hopefully, that will change when I'm located in a place of MY OWN! It also looks like living in the countryside of Babonneau spoiled me!

Tell Bill I love his little notes. Helps me know what he is interested in learning about. I bought an Eastern Caribbean cookbook yesterday. You'd love the meals.

I've heard from Caroline, Kathryn, Kathryn Beggs, Doris Dana, Pat Sakuhahn and today Belva. It is marvelous to get mail. Oh, yes, Janet, too! Take care of you. Love Mary Ann

I kept thinking, I've got to think of something intelligent to say, but not much of any substance ever came out. I kept thinking of so many of you and just knew you'd have no trouble at all conversing with this work figure while you sat in a chair dressed in a loose-fitting wrinkled housedress, flip flops on your feet and no bra! Right? I did manage to tell her I'd read she had brought about many positive changes to Dominica since she'd been Prime Minister and we talked about her buddy Ruth and her involvement with Peace Corp volunteers. I found Dame Charles very serious and intelligent and so gracious to accept my presence and talk with me for a few moments. I seems so far I'm the only PCV (58 volunteers) whose gotten to meet her. That puts me in an envious position. She left the following day for a three-week trip. I'm curious if she'll remember me at all, if I meet her again during the next two years.

Miss you all. Your support is just grand!

Love, Mary Ann
My new and permanent (two year) address is:
Mary Ann Kollenberg, PCV
Zicack Portsmouth
Commonwealth of Dominica, W.I.
Larger airfreight packages still get sent to:
P.O. Box 357, Roseau
Commonwealth of Dominica, WI

August 30, 1992

Dear Family and Friends:

Hot water is again a thing of the past! And I'm now a resident of Portsmouth, Dominic. Not that hot water and Portsmouth have any connection. It's just that after two weeks of hot showers in Roseau at Ruth's house on Cork Street, this morning's cold shower reminded me – I'm now on my own!

I wonder if I'll ever truly understand the value of having lived for all those seven weeks with West Indian families! They taught me so much. Most of the learning came gently and in the context of day-to-day living. But I'm also just as sure that I have no conception of the lessons still to be learned!

Melanie and I moved into our side-by-side, two-room flats yesterday morning. Such a big day! We'd shopped in Roseau all week for basic foods and household provisions because we'd been told things could be much higher in Portsmouth. At a casual glance yesterday afternoon, this appears to be true. So a weekly trip to Roseau may be in order for the future.

Each time I do something on my own – like open a bank account, buy an electric fan, fix a meal, shop, and travel to another village by myself – my confidence increases. I know exactly how Josh, Kyle and Kayla feel when they master a new "step." Often, these days I can feel the delight shown on Kayla's face the time she rolled over and over all the way across the family room floor. It wasn't from the fun of rolling, necessarily, but from the excitement of having done that for the first time all by herself!

House hunting was quite an experience. We looked at five places the first day and four on the second day. Portsmouth is an hour's drive from Roseau. The first day a driver from the Forestry Division brought us. The second day we came with the Peace Corps driver, Ryan, a Carib Indian. Both days were long, hot, tiring and discouraging. So by the end of the second day, both Melanie and I decided the two flats we'd seen the first day were not all that bad. Besides the landlord, a retired Dominican aircraft worker from London, had been working "diligently" fixing everything up. Earl Hector (the landlord) agreed to have things ready for us to move in on Saturday. And we both went back to Roseau, tired but content. We had a place to live!

Saturday morning was quite an eye opener. We arrived in Portsmouth with Earl still puttering about; screens to be put up, light fixtures to be covered, dishes to be gathered, tile to be fixed, gas to be hooked up, a chest of drawers and refrigerator to be bought. Lots has since been done and lots is still to be done and Earl is leaving for a month in New York come Tuesday evening! But that's life in the Eastern Caribbean.

I'm learning to be assertive and to negotiate at every turn. Fun for me! Our first night in the flat we chose to eat out and walked downtown (which is three streets of five blocks each) and ate fried chicken and French fries at the Cabin Restaurant. We watched a wedding party at the Catholic Church on the way and came home to a houseful of flying ants! These little creatures seem to be a cross between a gnat and a termite. They come out at night during the rainy season in search of bright lights. Solution – none! Actually, that's not true. Turn off the lights!

Now for the beauty. We are on a quiet street where we can see hills and the sea. It has been fairly cool (that word is relative) with beautiful clouds, lots of rain which washes everything clean. The people are friendly and happy to have us here. I have a small white table in front of my kitchen/living room window. The window is covered by a white lace curtain that I've tied back to reveal the sky and nearby hills. Our street, after it passes the park as a path, continues down to the sea, about three more blocks. Last night the sky above the Caribbean shone golden orange between the sea and a new moon. A young man named Morrison has befriended us and promises to show us around. Melanie may tutor him in reading in exchange for Creole lessons. Earl continually cautions us not to encourage the children or the animals – he has five dogs (two puppies) – or they "will become pests!" He's yet to mention to encouraging retired single men!

Still no concrete plan for our ENCORE work, but last Friday we met with the head man in the Forestry Division, Arlington James. The Division office is located in Roseau on the grounds of the Botanical Gardens. The ENCORE Peace Corps volunteers will be directly linked with the Forestry Division although our immediate supervisor will be a National Coordinator --- still to be hired. We (PCVs) can't commence work until she is hired. (They have a lady in mind).

I want to share with you my feeling on the meeting with Arlington James. Most of you know a lot about me. Some of you don't. But while I was taking night classes at college for all of 13 years, many people asked, "What are you going to college for?" I'd usually say, "I don't know yet. I just like to go to school." But through the years I learned more and more toward conservation. And when the time finally came, I enrolled in U.C. Davis as a Natural Resources major!

However, when I got to Davis, my advisor had just finished a survey of his graduates and he told me they were not getting jobs. So his advice was for me to change majors. I did and as most of you know I ended up with an Environmental Planning degree. But never quite lost the desire to work in Soil Conservation, Range Management, forestries or fisheries.

As I sat there, in the Dominican Botanical Gardens in an office of the Forestry Division, my mind looked back over all those paths that crossed and re-crossed so I could finally know another dream. Don't let anyone ever tell you, dreams don't come true!

Our biggest challenge now for we four PC ENCORE volunteers is to get to know our areas, the people, their problems, and let them know us. Saturday we plan a raft trip up the Indian River, next will be a hike through the Cabrits National Park with its ruins of Fort Shirley, a "probably" wet trek up Mt. (Morne) Diabiotins and maybe Mt. Aux Diables, plus I'm dying to see the rugged Atlantic Coastline of Dominica. And due north of Portsmouth are reportedly excellent snorkeling waters!

Speaking of snorkeling – I did! And, of course, during another confidence building experience. Snorkeling equipment was one of my main purchases before leaving home and I was anxious to try it out! The opportunity came last Thursday when an old-time PCV, Penny, offered to take four of us down her way to Scott's Head for a dip. Scott's Head is known world-wide (according to the tourist brochures) for its beautiful coral reefs, fish and clear water.

"Meet at the PC office at 12:30 and we'll take a transport down," said Penny. Penny is in her late sixties, a happy delightful woman who's been here a year now. She lives in Soufriere and teaches in Scott's Head.

When I arrived at the office, Penny and the others had gone! The secretary kept assuring me she just went out and would be back. But by 1:00 p.m. – no Penny; but Penny's Scott's Head school principal, Tyrone, bounded in asking for her – he'd offered her a ride to Scott's Head. After another ½ hour wait, Tyrone and I headed for Scott's Head on our own. He gave me a personally guided tour all the way down from Roseau, showed me all around his school (which he was extremely proud of), even asked if he could borrow me one day a week when I told him I was a vocational Ed teacher, then drove me out to the beach in search of snorkeling buddies. Poor Penny was beside herself when she saw Tyrone and me and realized she forgot us! But I was there, ready with mask and snorkel.

The actual land mass known as Scott's Head is connected to Dominica by a narrow spit of land that separates the Atlantic Ocean and Caribbean Sea. I still get a thrill over walking or driving along and looking one way to the Caribbean and one way to the Atlantic. Tyrone explained the sea waves were slowly eroding this strip of land – actually washing it away.

I must tell you, I'll never know why I've not snorkeled before. And we weren't in the best location – nor since it was my first try – did I go out very far. But I put mask and snorkel on, face in the water and became lost as I floated through an unknown world for over an hour! Black fish with bright yellow stripes, cobalt blue and turquoise, plaid fish, polka dotted fish, translucent fish with their skeletons showing through, and green on top, clear on the bottom, then reversed. The sun would strike their colors and I thought of the effervescence of the hummingbird. Mother Nature and God are incredible. I'm hooked!

I woke up the other morning in Roseau to the sound of a woman crying in the streets, "Ti-ti-wi, Ti-ti-wi," (pronounced "Tee-tee-wee). It turned out to be the tiniest of fish – minnow size – thousands are carried in a bucket and still attached to their jelly sacks. The ti-ti-wi was sold for $2.00 EC a cupful which the lady scooped out into the buyer's own container. Ruth bought some and cooked them up for lunch. Delicious! She simply steamed them with red pepper and curry in a cast iron frying pan. They turned from translucent forms with two eyes to tiny solid cream colored forms which resembled a small noodle. They're caught only during certain conditions – something like when the grunion run. The woman roamed the street for three days crying out her Creole words and then was gone.

Hurricane Andrew received headlines here on T.V. for days, as I know it did there. The Island people felt very akin to those in Andrew's path. They still remember their own 1979 David and less severe Hugo. I've yet to hear from any one of you about the fires, but they must also be devastating!

Last week I'd written in my journal, "My life has been reduced to the simplest form. I do the most basic things and the day passes; get up, breakfast, P.C. office for mail, shop, lunch, rest, write, walk, supper, shower, read. Wonder how long before I'll get bored?" The interesting thing is my tasks take total concentration and as long as that continues, boredom is not possible. Besides, on a moonlit night, you go on a swim and picnic on the beach. Put your face in the water and the moonlight lights up all the fish. At least this is how Paula, Ruth's young cook, explained it! I keep learning that whatever I do is okay! I don't have to move mountains, especially in this heat. Which reminds me, Portsmouth is much cooler.

One more story and I'll stop for this letter. Many of you have written. Thank you. I love hearing of life back home and keeping in touch with you. There are many questions when you write. Hope they eventually get answered.

Last Thursday evening Ruth, a friend of hers, and I had just returned from a trip through "Beverly Hills,' a spot just north of Roseau in the hills overlooking the sea and the Roseau Valley where the rich people live. Ruth has many buddies living up there and she proudly pointed out all their homes as we slowly drove by.

"Beverly Hills" is Ruth's terms, but the homes and gardens were impressive, to say the least.

About 7:00 p.m. there was a knock on the door (actually a woman's face appeared at a small front window from behind the curtain) "Good night," she said. Ruth opened the door. There stood an older West Indian lady licking a peppermint ice cream cone, dressed in a sun dress and sandals. She carried a small tub of butter under her other arm. Ruth pushed me out the door into the lady's waiting arms and said, "Take her to see my buddy."

I protested. "I've only my housedress on and no bra! I can't go like this." Ruth laughed and told me, "She'll probably be dressed the same!"

So the ice cream lady and I proceeded down the street to the end of the block where we waited in the dark for about five minutes until a long, brand new official car came slowly down the street and turned into the alley to park. Out got Dame Eugena Charles, sundress and all. She unlocked a side door, went inside, turned on lights and an air conditioner, then opened another door and walked into a small office. All the while, my ice cream licking friend was beckoning me to follow until I found myself shaking the Prime Minister' hand and sitting down in a chair opposite her desk while she checked over her miscellaneous correspondence. She offered me a ginger sweet and I was tongue-tied! I kept thinking, "I've got to think of something intelligent to say" – but not much of any substance ever came out. I did manage to tell her that I'd read she had brought about many positive changes to Dominica since she'd been Prime Minister, and we talked about her buddy, Ruth, and her involvement with Peace Corps volunteers. I found Dame Charles very serious and intelligent and so gracious to accept my presence and talk with me for a few moments. It seems so far I'm the only PCV – 58 volunteer who has gotten to meet her. That puts me in an envious position. She left the following day for a three-week trip. I'm curious if she'll remember me at all, if I meet her again during the next two years.

Miss you all. Your support is just grand! Love, Mary Ann

August 31, 1992

Dear Mom and Bill:

I'm actually sitting at a table writing, not propped up in bed! You'd think this letter would be neater, but doesn't seem to be.

I like living in Portsmouth. It is quieter than Roseau – at least on Cork Street. Last night Melanie and I took a long walk around the town and back up the hill to the side streets. It is so beautiful just before dark when all the coconut trees wave in the breeze and are outlined against the sky.

I' m taking photos and will get them printed and sent home sometime. It might take a month!

Also, saw a wrecked ship from Hurricane David and one from Hugo.

Your letters are great. Don't worry about anything you tell me. It is all part of life. Hope you're both fine. The fires just sound awful.

T.V.'s here now – so news will get less sketchy. I think my spelling is getting worse. I know my spelling is getting worse!

Take care. Thanks again for all the work on my letters. Hope it is worth it for you and all enjoy them. If not, please let me know how to improve.

Love, Mary Ann
P.S. Enclosing article that was in local paper. Somehow highlight new address message. Okay?

September 7, 1992; 9:30 a.m.

Dear Mom and Bill:

I'm waiting for Melanie, PCV from Virginia and my next-door neighbor, to get ready and we will go to town (Portsmouth) for our daily trek. We officially live in Zicack, but it is actually only three blocks to the post office and bank. So glad you have a map to follow. On my big Dominica wall map, Zicack is spelled Zicack. But spelling seems different all over. Many names derived from Creole – (Kweyol) which, as I've mentioned, is not a written language. Although, I understand they now have a dictionary.

September 7, 1992; 8:30 p.m.

Speaking of spelling – you are right. You and Caroline do a beautiful job in making my letters look so polished. I've even had comments on how nice they are. Someone wanted to know if I had my computer here! Thank you again for all the work. I do know how much everyone likes them. I'm the one getting the praise and thanks – never you two.

But I've decided it is just too much work to expect you to continue – not only that it will become expensive to continue at such a rate as I previously wrote. So I'll not write for a long while, maybe November. I'll just write to those who've been writing to me and continue to send my postcards – as long as I can afford them! I'll mention that to everyone I write to so they will know that and not be worried about my state of affairs!

Annette gave me a copy of Michener's "Caribbean." I got through the cruel parts, but I can't seem to finish it. I'm not sure whether it was Michener's book I didn't care for or the cruelty of it all! I did read a non-fiction book on the Caribbean by a different author. I enjoyed it – slaughter and all even though it was hard to understand civilized men doing what they were doing

Glad you can follow my happenings on a map. Enjoy Fort Bragg – or better yet – I hope you enjoyed Fort Bragg! I was thinking today, while swimming in the Caribbean Sea at Bell Hall Beach in Douglas Bay, that the sea connects a person to the whole outside world. Even though this is a tiny island – someone said it would fit inside Lake Tahoe – when you are on the beach looking out across the water and waves, the rest of the world feels close especially California or any other piece of land next to the sea.

Maybe at Fort Bragg you felt close to Dominica when you looked out over the ocean and maybe not!

Bill, thank you for your special notes. It seems the San Juan Puerto Rico temps are correct. And yes, the breezes make the humidity much less as does the shade and the sea – it was actually cool today! Swimming again tomorrow and a trip to a place up the road called Cottage.

Melanie and I are doing well together. She was raised on a farm in Virginia, is 22, just out of college, a very nice girl. I'm lucky to have her close by and to be working with her.

Take care. Thank you for the typed letter and your notes –

Love ya, Mary Ann

September 30, 1992

Dear Family and Friends:

A month ago today I sat at this same small kitchen table and wrote you my last letter. So much has happened during that time that I'll never get it all written down. But I hope I can give you some interesting highlights without losing the continuity of what's been going on in Portsmouth, Dominica, with this California PCU.

Before I get into a myriad of stories, may I once again thank you for all your letters! I've been trying to respond by sending cards, but I can't seem to keep up. Each one of you ask questions and I hope they eventually get answered. You'll be happy to know that "work" has commenced! So forgive me if this general letter is all you ever hear from me. Just remember, I relish each and every word you write and all the good wishes you send along.

Lori has developed three rolls of my slides and, so far, it looks like they'll tell a nice, visual story when I get home.

After all my words about house hunting in my last letter, Melanie and I plan to move. We'll still live in the village of Zicack, but around the corner and up the street. It is a brand new building – shop on the ground floor with a two-bedroom flat on the 2nd floor. Dominican Villages all have little shops spread through, on an average, one every two or three blocks. Most of them are in conjunction with the owner's living quarters. Items like beer, soft drinks, canned goods, candy bars; anything that the owner wants to buy elsewhere and resell is common fare. The shop can occupy a brand new building – such as the one below our anticipated new home –or be just a small wooden shed with a counter and shelves.

Finding this spot took some doing, but not necessarily on our part. Melanie and I have discovered the "Dominican Way," which means if you want something to happen, you simply think about it, and maybe talk about it and soon it will occur! We've also discovered if you talk to someone about locating a house for you, you give over total responsibility for house hunting to that person.

Our house hunter was a young, single parent named Cleetis. And, after a misunderstanding along with a miscommunication, we all got together to meet the owner. It's a beautiful place, much too good for Peace Corps volunteers! But rent is the same as our present location, the street is quiet, the school children and dogs have about done us in where we live now, and best of all, it has a front veranda and we'll be able to watch the sunsets over Rodney Bay!

Let me tell you straight out. Sunsets over Rodney Bay are the most incredible sights: The sun's receding rays, delicate and soft, seem to last for hours. Almost always the horizon above the sea is dotted with clouds in a long irregular line -- one night it resembled the skyline of a large city –between these deep grey clouds and the silver, lilac or golden sea, the sky may turn the softest of yellows. Above the grey clouds the pastel shade blends to pale orange. Then above all this beauty appear huge, tall grey-white billowing clouds still touched by the sun's rays from below. One night, beaming from these soft billows, there appeared two wide bands of pink, maybe one mile apart. These two pink stripes rose above the clouds straight up, and then were reflected in the water which slowly turned a silvery-lavender.

I know you think I'm exaggerating but I'm not. Melanie and I get laughed at all the time because we are always saying, "Oh, look at that! How beautiful!" We find design and color in everything, proclaiming our finds quietly to each other or loudly for all to hear. The locals (only some of them) tell us we'll get used to it all.

Just a few more words about our living quarters then I'll move on. Presently, Melanie and I live side by side in identical two-room flats or apartments. We share a common front veranda and a landlord who lives upstairs. We are directly across from the Portsmouth Government Primary School and everything, except for the dogs, was reasonably quiet until school started. Not only did the school children, who we love, become bothersome, but all the young men trying to get a glimpse of Melanie began to get on our nerves. With little sleep at night from barking dogs and a constant barrage during school hours, both Melanie and I became pretty frazzled and decided to put out feelers for a new and quiet spot. Our new place has two bedrooms, bath and shower (still no hot water, but that is now okay by me), kitchen, dining room, living room, front veranda, and a back yard space. The landlady says the shop won't go in for a long, long while. We've chosen to believe her.

Maybe I should describe Melanie. She is 22, sweet as can be with long curly, soft brown hair and brown eyes, beautiful lashes, and speaks with a perfect Virginian accent (drawl). She came by her accent legitimately by being raised on a cattle and tobacco farm in the Virginia hills. Any young man who desired to stop by our veranda during the first few weeks after we moved to Portsmouth had Melanie's undivided attention. Not that she had ulterior motives in mind, just that she is polite and wouldn't hurt a fly.

We've come to understand that we don't have to spend time talking to everyone! Especially if it's not convenient for us. There were, and still are, many times when my mothering instincts surfaced strong and quickly! When we first moved to Portsmouth we were taken for Ross Medical School students. That affiliation is not always a good one, so we would dispel the ideas quickly. But then we had to prove Peace Corps volunteers were different.

One night I was talking to two young boys, 14 and 15, on the front veranda. Melanie was in bed reading. Suddenly, a third young man jumped the veranda wall and stood face to face with me. I could smell alcohol on his breath as he confronted me with words like, "You've insulted us. Don't you know you're always supposed to show your face and not just talk through your window," et cetera, et cetera. He was about 19. I must admit I was very startled and apologized for whatever action he had taken as insulting, while I tried to figure out how I was going to get rid of everyone. After further confrontation, a car drove up across the street and two men got out and came over to the veranda wall. One, who had a nice friendly face, said, "What going on here?" I thought, oh, they've come to my rescue and replied, "I've been trying to get these young men to leave and have not had any success." The friendly man reached over and shook my hand and so did the other fellow who'd gotten out of the car. Instantly I did not care for him! But shook his hand, moved back and calmly (outside, not inside) said, "I'm going in now."

I turned, opened the door, went in, shut the door and locked it after me! I think about an hour went by before I stopped shaking. But both Melanie and I no longer feel we have to be <u>so</u> polite anymore. And the best part, the young man who confronted me is not so polite and only stops to say "good day," before moving on. We've both discovered our instincts are pretty reliable, but have decided we'll like living on a second floor much better!

Since my last letter, the Forestry Division and our local ENCORE site people have continued to treat us royally. Melanie and I took a canoe ride up the Indian River through the entwining mangroves, accompanied by Ken Roy, our Dominican guide, and his young apprentice, Willmouth. We've toured the Cabrits National Forest and Fort Shirley ruins where ground lizards of all sizes and colors charge across grassy areas or rustle under the fallen branches and leaves. The Cabrits and Ft. Shirley are a tremendous source of pride for the locals, and inhabit a small spit of land separated from the Portsmouth area by a swamp/marsh that is bounded on the south by Rodney Bay and on the north by Douglas Bay. Besides the ruins of its 18th century fort, the Cabrits contains two extinct volcanic cones, all kinds of exotic trees, trails and indescribable views. We've yet to hike to the top of either "hill" but will one day.

I think I've mentioned how much I like the lizards! They fascinate me, even the small ones on my ceiling above my bed!

In my quest to discover what Dominica is all about, nature-wise, we've gladly accepted offers to tour the island, swim in the Emerald Pool and drive (four-wheel) to Freshwater Lake and learn about the island's power system. There just isn't enough space here to explain Freshwater Lake and the power system, so that will have to wait until I get home. But "up on top" above the dammed-up lake is a track running from Roseau to Grand Pond, Roseau being on the west at the Caribbean Sea, while Grand Pond is on the east just in from the Atlantic Ocean! Freshwater Lake's elevation is close to 3,000 feet. In the days before roads, and on Dominica that is not all that long ago, the farmers of Grand Pond would rise about 4:30 a.m. or earlier and start walking to Roseau with their produce. Around 5:30 they would reach Breakfast River where they would meet up with other farmers from all over the region, have breakfast and continue from that point upward. They traveled in groups to discourage robbers. After reaching Freshwater Lake (then a natural lake) they traveled on relatively "level" ground for a number of miles before descending down, down, down into Laudat, Roseau Valley and finally Roseau where they traded or sold their items in exchange for provisions to take back home, back home being reached that same night!

The wind is fierce at Freshwater Lake, at least it was the day we visited. It blew mist across the water until we could no longer see, and in an instant blew it away again to reveal a green, stunted, windswept landscape and churning water. I thought I was in Scotland! Our guide, National Park Superintendent David Williams, did a beautiful job of describing how the farmers made their trek – we could feel their presence, determination and just plain "one step at a time!" David's driver, Houstis, also expertly negotiated a most precarious road with the Forestry Division's parrot green vehicle while the other three young ENCORE PCVs (not me) rode in the back! They got bounced, joggled, bumped, rained on, and windswept and never complained!

Each one of our treks so far has involved lots of driving mingled with a little hiking and some swimming. One such spot, the Emerald Pool, would have been the perfect salvation for California's hot, hot summer! Even though it's quite a tourist destination, the day we swam we had it almost to ourselves, probably because it was another rainy day, and if you can believe it, COOL! Goose bumps were common. We got soaked getting out of our suits back into our clothes and still had miles to go before getting home! That night I heated hot water for my shower and poured it all over me!

But the beauty and serenity of the Emerald Pool were worth ever shiver. On the Belle Fille River, my own guess from looking at the map, the Emerald Pool sits at the base of a free-falling, powerful waterfall where swimmers must be very strong to make their way behind the falling water. In contrast to the velocity and sound of the waterfall, the pool is framed on one side by a dripping, fern-covered cliff that's been naturally undermined to form a grotto. All around this idyllic setting hovers Dominica's lush tropical forest! Don't I sound like a tour guide? Anyway, if you don't get the picture that nature on Dominica is pretty spectacular, you can't say I didn't try.

ENCORE is becoming more and more alive. The government has hired a National Coordinator, Ophelia Maui, a well-known singer who until October 1st worked for the Tourism Division. She seems a special, capable lady. We've met her, but not for any length of time just yet.

For the last few weeks we've prepared and held a two-day workshop here in Portsmouth on ENCORE. The two PCVs at Scot's Head are doing the same. Our workshop was the 28th and 29th – theirs, today and tomorrow. The workshop was actually conducted by three fellows from World Wildlife Fund (WWF) in Washington, D.C. They are experienced in working with developing countries, although I'll say they really sweated blood over our Portsmouth workshop and not because it was hot! It was hot, lots of people came and all seems to have worked out well. The purpose of the workshop was to design a five-year strategic plan for ENCORE here at this site. If you can believe the main ENCORE group from St. Lucia and the Organization of Eastern Caribbean States (OECS) came en masse, secretaries and all, ordered computers, typed info in all during workshop – only, of course, until the power went out!

I absolutely love how the Dominican people interact, their vocabulary, their facial expressions, and their thought process. Both Melanie and I worked right along with the villagers helping put the ENCORE plan into place. The ease at which we were able to do this attests to the fact that all our previous interaction, getting to know people, "tiptoeing" so much, going slow, slow, slow is working. I'm not even sure that's what I want to say. But we felt accepted, and I can't explain what a marvelous feeling that is! Things could change tomorrow, and keep in mind, all the ideas generated at the workshop still must (or may) be put in place! I for one know just how much harder that is than simply being part of a workshop! But I have to tell you, I never dreamed my Peace Corps experience would include all this!

We still don't have an office, but work with the Local Site Manager, Thomas Paul. I'll tell you more about Mr. Paul in a future letter. But he has taken us under his wing and seems to cherish us. We've been working in his office, a small room next to his Cabin Restaurant adjacent to the North

River on the main street in Portsmouth. Both Melanie and I hope this situation will change, and besides his restaurant and catering business he tours guests who stay in his cabins around the island. He seems to be a community leader, is very religious and shares his ideas and thoughts on Dominica's natural beauty with us easily.

In preparation for the workshop, Mr. Paul scheduled a brain-storming session with other community leaders and members. There, for the first time, we met Rosie Douglas, Parliamentary Rep for the Opposition party, and finally a number of women! Both Mr. Douglas and a Mrs. Andre, local education officials, promptly discovered Melanie and I were single and just as quickly announced they'd have to find Dominicans for us to marry. Heaven knows how this will occur, but hopefully not in the "Dominican Way"!

We have a young friend, Luke, 29, who is our confidant, friend, companion on our swims in the Caribbean, and who keeps us both from missing home too much! Whenever we are a little down, along comes Luke asking us for a swim, to see a new part of the Island, to try a new food, or just to stop and chat awhile. Luke lives in Cottage, is married and has two young boys, Christan and Terron. Our intuition tells us Luke is special.

Speaking of special, last Saturday night the ENCORE PCV from Scotts Head, Chadwick, showed up in Portsmouth to spend the night. She'd driven up with two fellows, one who was the tour agent for an expensive, brand new sailing ship due in at the cruise ship berth about 7:30 p.m. Jackie, the agent, took us for a swim at the Purple Turtle Beach, bought us rum punches, let us shower and change, then took us on a tour of this sleek, white motorized sailing vessel built by a group of ten wealthy Frenchmen as an investment. The lifeboats alone, according to Jackie, cost $100,000!

Every inch of this ship was a thing of beauty, from the three massive sails as they lay folded at rest to its myriad of white ropes forming the frame for the sails when time came for uplifting! Not only did we tour the ship, on the following day, Sunday, Melanie and I, Mr. Paul, our other co-worker, Baldwin Baptiste, and the WWF people were checking out the workshop facility, not far from the cruise ship berth, when suddenly the ship began its departure. What a sight – late afternoon, sun setting, the sails slowly rising, ship moving in the water so it was broadside of us, the bay, and clouds and backdrop of green, mountainous, shadowed Dominica! Would you believe I had my camera? I did!

I keep trying to distinguish between what I think my Peace Corps experience should be and what it actually is. Of course, I have no choice but to accept it as it is, but luckily the Peace Corps Office has given us a booklet, "A Few Minor Adjustment," which helps me from feeling too guilty. Like last week when Lori sent me two boxes of items I couldn't bring with me initially. I was happy as a clam to receive them, but immediately felt bad for having so many things! I know the new house is going to affect me the same way. But I'm the only one it seems to bother. The villagers take it for granted. We are Americans and therefore rich! But I don't think trips to the Purple Turtle, rum punch, and sailboat boarding will become commonplace. At least not for Melanie and me. We've already decided that.

My heart goes out to you and all of those affected by the fires. You write, too, of sadness and of joy, of new things happening in your lives and of daily routine. It all interests me; just because I don't say that doesn't mean I don't care. I do. If I don't write again before Thanksgiving, have a happy one and think of me while you're gobbling turkey! We're having a Thanksgiving reception on the day following Thanksgiving where all us PCVs fix American type food and host a party for the nationals involved in Peace Corps on Dominica. It is by invitation only! We get to explain to them all about one of our National Holidays!

Love you all and miss you!

Mary Ann

P.S. Next time I should have a firm idea of the ENCORE projects to be carried out in Portsmouth and just how that will come about. (maybe!)

October 7, 1992

Dear Mom and Bill:

The nice people at the cruise ship berth keep giving me this information about ships that load in Portsmouth. I dutifully send them on to you, fully realizing that you've made your plans and they will stand. And all of it is okay. I think they feel bad because the ship festival is coming into Roseau and only for half a day!

Anyway, the lake and one (skip) is called the <u>Freewinds</u>! Don't you love that name? It is run by the Majestic Cruise Lines at 599-76900 in Curaco. Now how'd you like to fly to and from Curaco to take a cruise?

Caroline tells me that Annette and her friend George are taking a cruise to Aruba! It is so funny, because as of right now, I have no desire to travel anywhere. I'm sure that will all change, especially knowing my past history.

I hope you didn't get upset when this letter arrived thinking it was another general letter! But I'll try and hold off now until maybe Thanksgiving and make it a holiday <u>news from the Caribbean</u>. Kathryn Beggs is so worried I'll lose the continuity of my story telling if I don't write often! As I've mentioned to Caroline, all correspondence seems to be a problem, but I know it will sort itself out. I'm sure many people have written initially that won't write again. And I've written to a number individually and that may be what finally evolves.

But I must say it (the correspondence) has kept me on my toes and that has been good because of the "abstractness" of our jobs at present. The good 'ole American achievement and accomplishment syndrome lets me feel good when I get all my letters answered and mailed off! It's like a job I take very seriously.

Cooking is the same way. It allows me to be creative, learn more about the culture (foods and marketing), and best of all to feed myself. And, of course, I relish that! It seems eating properly in the heat is very important.

Before I forget, I'd love to have you tell me how many and which words I spell wrong in my next general letter because Lori sent me a dictionary and I'd like to believe lots of them are not spelling errors, but just the way I write! (handwriting)

So much seems to be happening at home. Or maybe it's because everyone writes and tells me news of sad happenings. Or are things really continually happening?

I got the nicest letter from Billie and Marshall. She tells no glasses for her. That much has been a blow. Especially if she felt they would help with her vision.

Well, off for now, Love Mary Ann
P.S. I bet San Francisco is lovely in fall! Thank you!

October 28, 1992

Dear Mom and Bill:

Your cards and notes have arrived from many places: Fort Bragg, San Francisco and Auburn. Kathryn Beggs writes how excited you are about the cruise and Lori tells me you stopped by. Hope you got to see Kayla! My prejudice, of course, but she must be a cutie-pie. Lori sends me photos and tells me she has four teeth; stands alone until she realizes this and promptly falls! Besides being a handful, do you know any second babies that aren't, Lori says she is a big girl! Takes after her daddy and grandpa maybe.

Enough of Kayla. Both Caroline and Lori tell me, too, of Kyle and Jeremy going to school together. Small world. I miss the kids and all of you and Caroline and K.G. Think of the fall coolness and it ensuing colors, of all the hustle and bustle and desire to run away that used to creep into my soul. Doris Vierra writes of a plaque dedication at Mt. Pleasant Hall. I'm waiting for her next letter to tell me how it went.

All here is on hold; actually, hold isn't the correct word, maybe stopped is better. Day-to-day happenings continue which means learning and learning and learning. But work, or better yet, the ENCORE project continues its illusiveness! Although we have meetings and write correspondence and meet people and discuss and discuss and move about (a local term). My personal opinion – only at this point and subject to change hourly – is that ENCORE is immersed in this web of bureaucracy which includes USAID, OECS (Organization of Eastern Caribbean States), WWF (World Wildlife Fund), the Government of Dominica; and each and every one of their regulations and requirements. If ENCORE succeeds or even gets off the ground down at the local community (village) level, it will be a miracle of historic importance! All said, of course, with tongue in cheek. But when monies given equal $11,000,000 U.S. and only $1,000,000 ends up "on the ground," as they are saying, for the actual money to be spent at the village level on Dominica – one does begin to wonder!

The most humorous side of all this for is – Didn't I join the Peace Corps to get away from all the bureaucracy? Another funny thing is I always end up in the field and just simply want to cut through all the red tape! But I've also been well trained to "play the game!" Life is life is life. My attitude is quite good today. Other days, this is not the case! Melanie is a dear. She keeps me afloat when the need arises and I've been able to do the same for her.

We've decided to take a house together, finally! It was off and on so many times (that seems to be the norm here), but yesterday we made a final decision. We hope to move on Monday. The move involves one and a half blocks! The house, I think I've mentioned before, is brand new; a front veranda faces the sea where we'll be able to watch the sunset over the village rooftops and look at the houses and hills bathed in evening light. We've dreamed of a second story – this is! We've dreamed of looking out and sitting out and having a sense of privacy, something we've not been able to accomplish at street level! So, with trepidation about living together, you know how I like my space, we hope to move Monday which is the day before Dominica Independence Day. This Friday is Creole Day and culture abounds. I'll write of all those experiences later.

Take care, Love Mary Ann

P.S. The house is actually too nice for Peace Corps volunteers, we think. But no one else seems concerned. They are more interested in our comfort. Isn't that nice?

November 4, 1992

2:30 p.m.

Dear Mom and Bill:

We've moved! It's a Day of Community Service. Yesterday was Dominica's National Independence Day – fourteen years, and I'm trying to catch up on my letter writing. I'm in possession of three nice letters from you all, so will start my stack with you. Thanks so much, again and again, for typing and sending off the last "News from the Eastern Caribbean." It's as much fun for me to get them back and read what I wrote as it is writing them and sending them off to you. I just read in the one and only Dominican paper that in order to have mail received by people in the States by Christmas it must be mailed by November 30. So I'll try to get a holiday type letter off sometime around 15 of November; then if you get it and deal with it by the Xmas time, all should work out fine!

I finally heard from Janie. That was nice. Also got your short card last week. Because of Independence Day, Creole Day on October 30th and Coney Com-la at Scott's Head and moving; Melanie and I have met ourselves coming and going. I hope to write about all in holiday letter, but I watched the lighting of the graves in Portsmouth Catholic Cemetery, I dressed in National Dress for Creole Day and for service yesterday for Final Vows for a local nun, rode to Scott's Head for Coney Come-la (blowing of the conch) on Saturday, rode and hitchhiked back from Scott's Head on Sunday, a true Peace Corps experience! And packed and cleaned my apartment in four hours. The body repelled but today it's resting, and our stove got hooked up this morning so I can eat something more substantial than sandwiches. Our <u>upstairs</u> flat is a block and a half from "old" place, still in Zicack. It's a two-bedroom, wing room, dining room combination and kitchen. But best of all, it has a veranda where we can sit or stand and talk to those who walk by; watch the sailboat and yachts in the bay over the rooftops of Portsmouth; look northwest to the Cabrits and southwest to the hills. Love it, love it, love it. So far (two days) living with Melanie seems fine. You know how I love my space. I'm sure we'll have our moments, but that's to be expected.

You are right. The price of your cruise is great. I hear it cost $1,300 just to fly here now during season! Thanks for article on Latitudes. I enjoyed it. Tell Bill though it's only been six months since we all ate there! Which in itself is a long, long time. I called Billie and Marshall on their anniversary! I talked to their <u>machine</u>! I'm anxious to get a note now from them about their reaction to my voice! Thanks for research on <u>Wordsworth</u>! I look forward to receiving all. Thanks too for spelling list. I made a few mistakes on place names that I'll correct next time. Rodney Bay is, for some unknown reason, know that way locally by a number of people, but officially it is Prince Rupert Bay and is labeled as such on that map! I evidently learned from the locals and did not check on it. Also, Grand Pond turns out to be Grand Fond or Grandfond! My main boss' name is Ophelia Marie not Maui (page 4). I'm looking forward to your visit. It will be here before we know it. I have a few places for that morning and will share them with you to see how you feel about them.

Take care, M.A.

November 14, 1992

Dear Family and Friends:

Happy Thanksgiving, Merry Christmas and Happy New Year!

By the time you receive my greetings, Thanksgiving will be over and Christmas right on your heels. I've been hearing that Christmas here is a very quiet time. No such things as presents, parties or Christmas trees. Melanie and I are thinking of having a tree and maybe a small get-together. For Thanksgiving, the Peace Corps Volunteers are all holding a big open house at the Peace Corps office in Roseau. We've given out invitations to 200 people, some VIPs at the government and ministry levels, but mostly at the personal village level.

Melanie and I handed out our invites yesterday. We were given five each, but combined them and gave out nine to very special friends and co-workers. The recipients were so thrilled it just warmed our hearts. We're serving such things at the Open House as ham and turkey sandwiches, pumpkin bread, quiche and rum punch! I understand the punch always goes over the best!

In your many letters you express the desire not to miss out on any of my experiences. Be absurd that much of the time is spent in a daily ritual of rising, eating, walking to work or to shop, making phone calls, doing laundry, reading, talking and sleeping. I mustn't forget taking a shower! Dominica's weather has changed! This is now the cool season and will last from November through February. Breezes are cool, nights almost <u>chilly,</u> clouds cover much of the sky day and night, nights bring heavy· rain storms, and energy abounds -- not only in the bodies but also in the clouds. Lightning often lights up the whole sky. One evening, about an hour after sunset, we watched a huge dark grey cloud far out at sea light up like the U.S. Navy was carrying on a battle on its far side. Anyway, you can imagine how an early morning cold shower now feels. I've moved my showering time to evenings and last night heated water to pour over my shivering body. I even get goose bumps at the beach - not on the sand, but definitely in the water.

Some of you have also asked for a recipe or two and for me to describe the reality of my Peace Corps experience versus my expectations. I've enclosed two recipes: Pumpkin Soup and Green Fig (Banana) Salad. The pumpkin soup is my favorite so far (that I cook), and the salad (when made by a West Indian) tastes just like potato salad!

GREEN BANANA (FIG) SALAD

6 young green bananas	1 clove garlic, crushed
1 lime (juice only)	1 onion, grated
¼ hot green pepper	1 Tbsp. salt

Cook banana in salted water (with skins on) and a little lime juice (about 1 tea-spoon) until tender, but NOT TOO SOFT. In bowl put crushed garlic, salt, hot pepper, lime juice and onion. Add 1 ½ cups boiling water and allow to stand for five minutes, keeping warm. Then peel bananas which have already been cooked and put into sauce. Allow to stand for one minute and serve while hot. Note: each cook seems to add their own extras to salad. Be creative.

PUMPKIN SOUP

1 pound pumpkin	4 cups stock (ham hock)
3 Tbsp. butter	¼ cup shredded ham
4 Tbsp. water	1 Tbsp. grated onion
Salt and pepper	

Peel and cut pumpkin into pieces. Cook in 3 Tablespoons butter and 4 Tablespoons water and salt to taste. When pumpkin is soft, crush and pass through a sieve. Dilute puree with 4 cups of stock. Add ham, pepper and onions. Allow to simmer for ten minutes over low heat. Note: I cook pumpkin in water and mash all together then add potatoes and carrots (sliced). These can be cooked to help thicken the soup, also. Again, be creative. West Indian pumpkin is often green and yellow striped and has the consistency of acorn squash.

As far as reality versus expectations, that would take reams of paper to describe; and hope-fully letter by letter some of that comes through to you. For now, one-sixth of the way into my two-year experience, I can say there is almost no connection between the two. At home, on River View Drive, I worried about so many things that never materialized; but I had no concept of how difficult it would be to sever all my emotional ties and let those relationships evolve to a different level - no better or worse -- but just as beautiful as they were in Auburn. I've always liked people, but again I had no idea that the Dominican people would be so proud, full of love, trusting, friendly, beautiful, intelligent, and diverse. Living all my life where one culture - mine - was dominant gave me no insight into living in or about the behavior of another culture where a different race is dominant. This is their world; they know how to survive here and live here and be happy; how to dress, to communicate, to work and play. Many people I talk with are more aware of the changes occurring in the World than folks at home. They also know the huge gap that they must span to catch up. Dominica has been described as California in the 1950s. So try to imagine that scene coupled with the introduction of computer technology without benefit of the last 40 years for transition.

On a personal level my greatest frustrations, at this point, involve making decisions on going to the beach, to parties, and what to wear! I do <u>not</u> miss TV, driving a car, or the telephone; although, I think now that we've moved we'll be getting the latter. I discover more and more how important it is to just think of today and let tomorrow take care of itself. I read this morning that "When the desire to pursue a particular avenue keeps presenting itself, we should pay heed, trusting that we will be shown the way to succeed." Even though I don't believe in 'shoulds', I believe that statement to be true.

Enough philosophizing for now except I want to share our favorite sayings with you: No. 1. "We came here to learn, so there'll be no getting upset when something happens that helps us learn!" No. 2. "If you have doubts, don't do it!"

Melanie and I have moved into a new home and work is progressing smoothly. At work, we develop monthly work plans which almost always get completed about halfway through the month, because it is next to impossible to plan a month in advance! We are trying to set up an office (no building yet), order furniture, supplies, and equipment including a computer! I actually called around, got prices, and developed a budget and discussed computer equipment and quotes. Then we put all on paper only to find out that most of it will be centrally purchased at the Ministry level. Who knows when that will be, but lo and behold they now have prices, a list of supplies and a budget compliments of the Portsmouth "office." The ENCORE Project on Dominica is structured through the Ministry of Agriculture to the Forestry Division with a National Coordinator and a National Coordinating Committee to a Local Site Manager (our Boss - Thomas Paul) in Portsmouth and a local Site Management Team. And I thought the Peace Corps was bureaucratic! It is going to take (has taken) forever to get things done. We learned Thursday that our National Coordinator, Ophelia Marie, must approve all our documents and concur with all of our activities. (Speaking of expectations versus reality.)

Portsmouth, though, even with all of its problems - drugs, unemployment, and perceived National Government neglect – is 100 percent behind ENCORE. We've selected the Local Site Management Team, have held three meetings and a big Strategic Planning Workshop; Thomas Paul has attended a ten-day "Co-Management for Sustainable Development" seminar, written three draft project proposals, and met with the Indian River "Boys" (tour guides) to help them form an official group. The Indian River "Boys" are fascinating. Most of them are school drop-outs, incredible competitors for the tourist dollar and river-wise! They live in a world all their own yet earning good money guiding local and foreign tourist up the Indian River. Hopefully, once they get organized,

ENCORE will help pay for tour guide training, brochures, "uniforms", motors that don't pollute, and a plan to keep the river clean.

In my never-ending quest, to understand all of the details of every project I'm involved in, I ask a myriad of questions, and slowly the plan or ideas begin to evolve. Thomas Paul is very patient with me and lets me ask away. The other day he said, "Kollenberg, it's not that you aren't smart, it's just that your mind uncoils very slowly." We all get along very, very well: Thomas, Melanie, Joanne, the typist, and I, our workdays vary – some days 8:00 to 12:00, some 8:30 to 1:00, some 8 to 5, and some 9:00 to 10:00! There is absolutely no consistency, and we can truly never predict a day's outcome. For instance, Thursday I waited two hours to set up an appointment to meet with the Catholic priest: Melanie and I are going to study, under the guidance of Father LaEluer, all about the Catholic Church. Friday three phone calls interspersed throughout the day to find out Ophelia Marie had left the Island and wouldn't be back until Tuesday. . . Only seven out of 29 of the Indian River "Boys" bothered to come to the organizational meeting even though Thomas drove out to the River to talk to them. But just then some tourists arrived and the three o'clock meeting didn't start till close to four.

But, for the most part, I find the unpredictability okay because when I pull a "boo-boo" it's not too serious.

So that you don't think I work too much, I'll change the subject for a while. Remember when it seemed like all I did was play? Now trying to set up a field trip to one of the project sites takes lots of organizing. Also, our friend Luke's pick-up "died." Thomas sideswiped a pole and his pick-up spent 2 weeks in the shop. It's amazing how activities slow down without wheels. But we've been OCCUPIED in moving, adjusting to our new "digs" and street, Independence Day and Creole Day activities, trips to Roseau on the transport, and meeting new people!

One day we spent some time talking to one of our young friend's mother. Loick (pronounced Lou Week) is eight years old and his Mom, Eunella, is about 30. She, her family of three boys and husband Paul, live in a small wooden house close by where we lived first across from the government school. We've moved around the corner from our old apartments, a block and one-half away into the same second story flat I described in my last letter. Before we moved, Eunella told us how she'd gotten married and moved to Portsmouth when she was younger. She said she was born and raised in Thibaud on the Atlantic Coast, eight miles away. She said, "I'd sit in the little house there and cry my eyes out from missing my family so much and being sick for home." Melanie and I empathized but really had no understanding until our recent move. Our block and one-half move opened up a whole new world, new faces, new neighbors, a loss of old familiar faces, a new way of walking to town, views of the Caribbean and its sunsets, and a sense of freedom. We felt oh, so guilty before we moved; it is a nice, nice place. But come to find out, our friends and co-workers are happy for us because they want to see us happy and well taken care of. The hardest part - besides physically moving - has been the loss of our young friends in our old neighborhood. We walked that way the other day and saw Loick. He looked up at us, put his arms around Melanie's waist, and said, "I missed you!" Then he turned and hugged me just as tightly. We also miss the lizards!

Last week at a Saturday night Portsmouth Cultural Gathering, we met a 1989-90 Peace Corps

Volunteer who'd been stationed in the Marshall Islands. She came by today and her first words were, "You aren't Peace Corps Volunteers!" But we convinced her it was okay to live like this.

For Independence Day and Creole Day Melanie and I had National costumes made. The costume is called a Jupe. According to the local paper, "The first true Creole dress was worn by free women on Sundays and feast days. This floor length skirt is of bright colours over a white cotton chemise with ribbons threaded through the lace at the neck and sleeves. A white handkerchief, later replaced by madras, was wrapped around the head while a coloured cotton triangle or foulard was draped over the shoulder completing the resemblance of a whole dress." The skirt is pulled up on both sides showing the ribbon and lace decorating the under garment. Our neighbor explained this practice was begun to show how rich you were in the days when almost everyone was poor. All they could afford was ribbon and lace for the slip.

On Creole Day, Melanie and I wore our costumes all around town. The locals just loved it. They'd beam and say, "Thank you for honoring our National Dress." We'd been told there is too much to do during the Independence time. We are now true believers of that statement. On Friday, all the schools had Creole Day programs. We walked around town looking at everyone else's dress. The school children, all dressed in costume, marched through town. The men's National Dress is black pants and shoes, a white shirt, black tie and red sash at the waist. The women's outer skirts are made of mostly red, yellow, orange and green plaids. The combination of the boys' and girls' outfits was magnificent. At noon we ate a traditional Creole meal: Codfish, roasted breadfruit, smoked (land) crabs and cucumber salad prepared by the mothers of the local pre-school.

The following day we headed for Scotts Head to celebrate their Coney Cone-la, spent the night in Scotts Head with another Volunteer, and had a true Peace Corps experience getting back home to Portsmouth on Sunday! Coney Cone-la, the blowing of the conch, is basically a street dance accompanied by all manner of barbecued fish and chicken, and drinks. On Sunday morning, the only day transports don't run on a regular basis, we were up at 7:00 a.m., after getting to bed at 2:00 a.m., and with a new friend from Scott's Head named Keegan, we headed out to catch a transport home about 10:00 a.m. What an experience it turned out to be. Melanie and I didn't have a clue what was in store for us. We did know we'd been advised not to travel on Sundays, but I believed we'd get home, how didn't matter. Remember the "Dominican Way?"

About 10:15 we caught a transport at Scotts Head going to Roseau, then a second one from our stopping point in Roseau to Mahaut fairly soon. In Mahaut we had time to buy a slice of watermelon (cold, red and juicy) before catching another transport to Saint Joseph. There we were let off at the corner to sit alongside the road - thank heavens in the shade. We sat for almost an hour! Finally a young man in a pickup took us another 10 miles. When he dropped us off we were picked up by a fellow in a small Toyota who took us all the way to the turnoff for Coconut Beach about four miles from Portsmouth. We started to walk and realized we hadn't eaten. We were ever so thirsty so we stopped at the Portsmouth Beach Hotel where we ate lunch and walked home along the beach: not as easy as it sounds. We crossed a river mouth, climbed over rocks, gravel and garbage, and even walked through paths in the thicket when the beach became inaccessible. Hot, tired and sore-footed, we got home just in time to shower and dress to attend the blessing of our soon-to-be new home! We'd left Scotts Head at 10:15 a.m. and arrived in Portsmouth at 3:30 p.m. Thank heavens for Keegan, and it'll be a long time before we travel on Sunday again! Keegan, like so many of our friends, is special. He tells us, "I think whatever you want to do for you is best! If that makes you happy, then I am happy.

The next day, Monday, we were invited guests at the annual youth rally in downtown Portsmouth at Borough's Square. Five schools sent all their students, ages eight and up, marching in full school uniforms to the Square where they stood at attention listening to speeches in the hot morning sun. No one fainted and luckily for the children, clouds and rain passed over to cool everyone off! As if all these activities weren't enough, we'd chosen Monday to move. So between 1:00 p.m. and 5:00 p.m. I packed and cleaned my apartment. We'd arranged for a friend and a pickup to move us, we thought. But neither arrived, so we carried enough over ourselves to spend the night in the new flat. Then the next morning we walked back and asked our old landlord if he'd move us. He graciously did! He had both the old flats rented out again within two day!

Independence Day, Tuesday, Melanie wanted to go to Roseau to see the big military parade and Cultural gala but she couldn't get me back on a transport. I find riding to Roseau, walking around, visiting, shopping or doing business and then riding back to Portsmouth one of the most exhausting things I do! I usually start out fresh first thing in the morning, and the ride down is cool. I try to get a window seat and watch the sea and feel the breeze all the way down. But by the return trip, hot and tired, the drivers pack us in tight along with our purchases. Then it's seldom a straight trip home - many detours are made; through town to pick up packages too heavy or too many to carry to the bus stop, stops to pick up promised passengers or to drop off packages for friends. On the return trip the sun glares off the Caribbean directly on the transport and the drivers are in a big hurry to get home. On a recent trip Melanie said, "I was crammed in so tight for so long, parts of me went to sleep that I didn't know could go to sleep!"

Oh, yes, on Independence Day Bill Clinton won! We've heard such interesting comments on America's political going on. It was fun being here to see it all from such a different detached perspective. On Tuesday, besides sitting in our new home and wondering who was winning the election, Melanie and I attended services for a local lady saying her final vows to become a nun. We got to the church at 3:30. The service lasted until 7:30! Four hours on hard wooden benches. Most of the audience including us were dressed in national wear. There was such beauty and love in that church; fresh flowers, madras (bright plaid) material decorating the walls. Ophelia (our National Coordinator) sang, there must have been 25 priests, numerous nuns, two choirs, the offerings of food carried down the aisle by people in national costume, a dance group all dressed in green and blue, many songs done in harmony by visiting priests, always accompanied by a guitar. The young woman who took her final vows that day was born on Nov. 3, 1961, so it was her birthday, and she also dressed in national wear. Two of the priests who helped carry out the ceremony were her lifelong friends. I felt honored to be able to watch the service. It was one of the most moving ceremonies I've ever seen.

We still count our blessings almost daily. The other day, after we'd moved, a neighbor lady stopped us in the street and said, "I've been watching you and the way you conduct yourselves. You fit into Dominica and our ways very nicely. I like that very much." Then she moved on, didn't elaborate. But that, too, is the Dominican Way - straight and to the point - no extra words!

Last weekend 200 folks from Guadalupe came to Portsmouth to take part in a cultural evening, tour the Island, and challenge Portsmouth in football (soccer). The Frenchmen won 4-0. The cultural evening got off to a late - 9:00 p.m. - start, and Melanie and I lasted until 2:00 a.m. We'd been there, at Borough's Square, since 6:30 p.m. Dance/performing groups came from all over the Island including the Carib Territory. The costumes and drums were worth the whole evening to me. Luckily we found seats on a hotel balcony instead of standing - probably why we could make it until 2:00 a.m. We heard the next day it had been a good time to go home. About 3:00 a.m. a fight broke out involving 15 guys. Dominicans get rough when they drink too much! During the course of the evening Melanie had a number of young men approach her. Their lines are quite original, and they desperately wish she could or would get rid of me! It's so funny to us now, because we feel uncomfortable talking to white people but not to West Indians. It's like we think we stick out when we're talking to or hanging around other white people! We must have adjusted!

I must mention again how much I love your letters. They keep me connected. Have a Merry Holiday.

Love and miss you! Mary Ann
P.S. In my last letter Rodney Bay should have been Prince Rupert Bay! Sorry about that! I've now taken five rolls of slides! Just like letter writing, I'll probably slow down on that for a while too. The National Coordinator, Ophelia Marie, teases Thomas Paul about taking us to Roseau to work for her. He gets pretty upset!

November 15, 1992

Dear Mom and Bill:

This might be the test of tests for you to transcribe the enclosed letter! Best of luck and thank you so very much. If the recipes mean an additional page, please just put a note somewhere and say they will come next time or something. You'll be happy to know it is getting harder and harder to find time to write my long letters. But I'll never know when down the road the spirit might move me again. I write in my journal and try to keep answering all the people who write me. Crazy! When we work during the week, our only time is Saturday and Sunday. What else is new? It is also fun to get involved in things here such as church and church activities. Amazing how the time goes by. I also love reading and just sitting on the veranda watching! Laundry is a constant as is meal preparing, walking here and there. I love the Saturday market, and am getting better at finding what I want. This Saturday, yesterday, I bought spinach, sweet potatoes, pumpkin and bananas. The goods are all sold from the sidewalk, out of pick-up beds, or inside a building on the floor or high counters. The market is pretty good size but nothing like Roseau's.

Thanks again for all the work and help in keeping the "audience" apprised of my P.C. experience!

Love, Mary Ann

I heard a very revealing story about a Dominican PCV who was in the group that left the Island when we arrived. The story goes like this: It seems PCV underwear gets quite a workout what with hand laundry and constant wear over a two-year period. Given that set of circumstances, just before a volunteer is due to return to the States, his or her (in this case her) underwear is pretty precarious. So it happened that one day Ms. PCV was walking down a Roseau street when the elastic in her panties lost its last ounce of strength allowing them to slip to the sidewalk just around her ankles. Using her skill, training and P.C. ingenuity, she stepped out of her underwear and casually continued on down the street.

December 12, 1992

Dear Mom and Dad:

I'm in receipt (as they say with the business world) of three letters, a postcard and a Xmas present from you all! And no doubt soon I'll receive another package (hope) and a letter with my typed general letter in it: I hear through the grapevine that the last one is out. I called Lori this morning and she said she enjoyed it. Her comment was, "It was fun!"

Your postcard about tape is cute. Small or large, any tape will be appreciated. Funny, Bill's Xmas present arrived first! I have it on the shelf (our Xmas tree for now) alongside Melanie's four! I'm doing a tape to send home. Hope to get it off on Monday! It's been fun to do – hope it's not off too long or boring. I'll send it to Lori and she will no doubt sent it around.

Bill's comparison of ENCORE's cost to a B-36 helped a lot. You are right, and luckily, no cost overruns on the project. One would never do that in the West Indies (if they were smart). In fact, I've often wondered why they do it anywhere.

I can't predict weather for February. I do know a big Club Med boat came in yesterday and everyone got soaked! But maybe they enjoyed the experience. I sure do

Your November 5 letter had an incredible comment, "But we do have a new President, Bill Clinton. Is this important enough for the Caribbean to know?" Hope to shout it is. I'm afraid the local Dominican people know more about what goes on in the word than most Americans. They are very interested in America because many of them have relatives there and plan to travel there or even hope to move there. They are also very religious – so Bush was a favorite because of his anti-abortion stand. And for some reason, they (lots of them) really liked Bush.

Your travelling's to Billie and Marshall, et cetera, sound good. I keep in touch with them and I like that. Glad you sent photos up. One day (soon?) I'll have some more. No, I don't need pocketbooks at this point. Thanks. Language was a bust for me. I've never picked up anymore and as of now, it's not needed at all for my work or day to day. Some younger ones have picked it up good (well). And Melanie is working on it slowly. Did learn recently that if you speak Creole you can probably understand French and vice versa, but if you speak patois you have no clue about French. So instead of being the same thing – they (Patois and Creole) are like two different languages.

So sorry about Bill George not doing well after his fall. It makes me sad that he has to go through this now after the cancer. Let me know, too, how Bill's consultation is on December 18th.

Plans for February 17 may include a ride around Roseau and up to Giraudel then back to Roseau and up to Trafalgar to see falls and have lunch. Then back to boat. My plans depend on the transportation. I don't think I can afford to rent a taxi or hire a transport. So am looking to ask a friend with wheels or get a driver and rent a car. Giraudel would take you up a mountain, Trafalgar would show you a deep canyon and waterfall; plus, there is a special spot to eat at the falls – but it might be too full on Cruise Ship Day – oh, well, in Dominica all is flexible, I'm learning!

Love and thanks in advance for next issue of general letter.
Merry Xmas M.A.

January 1, 1993

Dear Mom and Bill:

I've put off writing to you because I kept thinking the shipping taxes would come and I could tell you it arrived safely and thank you and also my copy of the "general" letter. But no such luck, and I have the time and desire to catch up on my correspondence – so there! How's that for a reason to write? Just joking, of course!

You won't believe this, I know. But your Christmas card came via Lori. You had mailed it to 323 River View Drive, Auburn, California, 95603. The Auburn Post Office had forwarded it to 1470 Burlin Way, Auburn, California, 95603. Lori sent it to me in my Christmas package that arrived the day before Christmas. I guess when you have a daughter that keeps moving and changing addresses so often (five in the last year) it is very hard to keep track!

Bill's ornament arrived quite a long while ago and for weeks was my only Christmas present among Melanie's many. But then Bob Morelli sent me a gift of lots of goodies (calendar, Peace Corps batch, poster, magazines); Janie sent her calendar; Lori a rolling pin, pie tin, knife and spatula; and on and on. You probably know how my list got divided. Then yesterday I received three more packages – one from Patty and Mark Fowler full of everything from cookies to paper clips! Now I feel too favored and overwhelmed! No happy medium. Nancy Crouch even sent me a Christmas night shirt – snowflakes and all. I've also been getting pictures from people: Grandkids, Kathryn's desert photos – my heavens she takes good pictures, hikes some friends have been on. So as you can see, I'm in no way deprived – but blessed (as usual).

Bill, your ornament was lovely. Thank you. We didn't have a tree, but the ornament will always have special meaning – besides being pretty – it's the first Xmas present I got in Peace Corps!

Melanie and I have made it to Martinique to spend day with Barb Dawson from 49er R.O.P. She and family on a cruise and her closest port of call was Martinique. She brought us a blender to make juice! Also, they treated us to a taxi tour, lunch, shopping and hours' worth of talk! We got there at 9:00 a.m. and met then at 10:00 a.m. – they sailed (wrong term) out at 5:00 p.m. We left for airport at 3:30. So it was a nice long day! Made me think more of the day when you'll be here. I sort of put myself in your shoes while I was on Martinique.

I'm worried about Bill putting off his operation, but all your reports indicate that is not a problem. Please, please don't hesitate to change your mind if it is. So sorry about Uncle Reid. I was glad it was Kathryn who told me. I'll miss him very much as I know so many others will, too. I got a Christmas card from Ann Renz. She sounds as young as ever. We spent the day after Christmas with a lady (elderly) and met her brother who is 86. He had been to Roseau for the holiday. Any 86-year-old that can take that trip is a young 86. A number of people, Kathryn and C included, have sent me fall leaves. They were still perfect when they arrived. Nice, nice touch.

I hope to get another "general" letter off sometime before the end of January.

Bet you are excited about the trip. Barb Dawson could not get us on her ship! So we won't count on that. Hers was five stories, two elevators and held 1,200 people. HUGH!

Take care and enjoy Janie's visit.

Love you, Mary Ann
P.S. Uncle Johnny sent his booklet on Sacramento Museum. I sure am enjoying it.

January 3, 1993

Dear Family and Friends:

We now have a telephone (1-809-4445-4891) at home and a computer at work! I'm in the Peace Corps? You won't believe my reaction to the computer! It seems the ENCORE Project on Dominica was not set up to accommodate a secretary at the local sites, only at the National Headquarters in Roseau. Translated this means, "The Peace Corps are capable of doing all that." So even though boss Thomas Paul had gotten permission to have a secretary for a short while, about mid-November we had to let her go. Now, this wasn't quite as bad as it sounds for Joanne (a lovely, quiet young lady of twenty-two) even though we all hated to lose her, she's since taken a job for a local lawyer. But Joanne had a typewriter! It was sent to her by her father from Connecticut, had a memory, daisy wheel and all. There's no such thing as a rental typewriter in all of Dominica!

Just imagine three busy people: Thomas, Melanie and Mary Ann with letters to write, minutes to complete, reports and work plans to submit, everything with a cc: National Coordinator Ophelia Maria! By the time the rental computer came, Melanie was real tired of printing! (She writes the most legible of the three of us.) So when we finally got the computer installed by a local firm known as A.O. B. Rent-A-Comp, we'd been saving paperwork for almost a week in anticipation of the big day. After the initial learning and getting used to it all, I typed in my first document, saved it and waited, decided to make some changes and tried to move from the beginning of the document to the end. It took FOREVER! I turned to Melanie and said, "My heavens this computer is slow!" Then we both burst out laughing.

It seems I'd gotten used to and accepted lots in my five months on Dominica. But this was my first experience with a computer since I'd left home. A computer, to me at least, still meant speed. I believe somewhere in this lesson is what the Peace Corps meant when they wrote, "Being assigned to the Eastern Caribbean will not be as hard physically as going to another country (that's what they think); however, the psychological challenges will be far greater than most other Peace Corps assignments. You may often fall into the trap of believing you are in a modern country instead of a third world country."

Christmas Eve at 4:00 p.m. found both Melanie and I, minus Thomas Paul, attending an Indian River Tour Guide Association meeting on the banks of the Indian River. The Christmas season in Dominica brings out the tourists. They come in yachts, cruise ships, and airplanes. I've yet to see anyone swim in, but you never know. Keep in mind, when I say tourist, on Dominica it doesn't necessarily mean a white person. Most of Portsmouth's tourists visit from the neighboring island of Guadaloupe. As we met with the "boys" who are the tour guides that take the tourist up the Indian River (and who are now "organized" into a formal association thanks to some of our efforts and some of our mistakes), the surrounding hues of reds, blues, oranges, yellows, and the ever-present island green reflected in the water in the late afternoon sun. The Indian River empties into the Caribbean Sea just a few feet from our meeting spot. It felt good to be there. The "boys" treat us special and seem honored by our presence. In fact, if we don't show up for a meeting they feel slighted, and we hear about it!

Tomorrow, after a week and a half off, it's back to work. Besides Christmas and New Year's, for me this mini-vacation included a trip to Martinique, an overnight stay in the Carib Indian Territory, Boxing Day, and a Merchant's Holiday. Not bad for Dominica's very quiet holiday season. I attended Midnight Mass on Christmas Eve, then (along with Kenroy and Melanie) stayed up till 3:00 a.m. opening presents and drinking sorrel juice (a bright red, traditional drink made from the petals of the sorrel plant flower with sugar and cinnamon added). On New Year's Eve, I opt for bed and went instead to Mass on New Year's Day. If 1993 is anything like Portsmouth's New Year's Day Mass conducted by Father Reggie, it's going to be smashing!

Melanie and I'd been invited to visit four homes for Christmas Day, plus a fifth home on the day following Christmas known locally as Boxing Day. There are numerous stories about why it's called Boxing Day. One, kind of far-fetched but nevertheless repeated story says Boxing Day is when all the men wear the new boxer shorts they got for Christmas and couldn't put on during Christmas Day because the family was always standing around and there was no privacy to change.

Just in case someone might also drop by our house on Christmas Day, Melanie had made sorrel juice, and I bought a fruitcake. If we ever get the oven fixed, I'll make my own – hopefully by next Christmas! We'd also made oatmeal (no-bake) cookies to take as gifts to each house. Our only company, Luke and Earl, came just before lunch. After serving them our holiday fare, a bite to eat – wrong move – and Melanie and I were off to visit Mrs. Andre, Mrs. Valerie, Mrs. Green, and Kenroy's family. Luckily for the waistline, we only made two houses!

Mrs. Andre, a generous, happy, outgoing woman of also generous proportions, welcomed us with open arms. After visiting her one day on a work-related project, I returned to the office and announced, "I now understand why it's such a treat to be hugged by a fat lady!" When she hugs Melanie, she lifts her right up off the ground. On Christmas Day, Mrs. Andre rolled out a serving cart lined with various bottles filled with red and green drinks including rum and vodka to be added to the drink of our choice. The highlight of our visit to Mrs. Andre's turned out to be Goat Water (goat mutton cooked with vegetable – delicious), recipe enclosed!

We turned down cake at Mrs. Andre's and moved on to Kenroy's house where we did eat cake and drank more sorrel juice. Later, we discovered Mrs. Green wasn't home, and since it was getting dark, we decided against stopping at Mrs. Valerie's. Lucky choice! When we arrived back at our front steps, the young neighbor man, Bat, invited us into his modest home. We were amazed! He had a bottle of champagne, homemade cake, wine and sliced apple all served up on placemats on his living room coffee table. Bat is only 19, and we were not only impressed, we felt quite special as we were his only guests for Christmas Day. Sharing photographs had been the correct thing to do – at each house we were treated to album after album after album.

I realize by the time this letter reaches you, the holidays and maybe even January will be a thing of the past. But I beg of you, listen to just one more holiday "food" story. This one involves Miss Savarin, an 80+ year old single, Dominican lady living in Portsmouth in a spacious flat above her book and stationery shop. Arriving at 2:30 p.m. (Miss Savarin had invited us to spend some time with her on Boxing Day earlier in the week), we were first shown round her flat from top to bottom to back yard and garden, then offered (what else) sorrel juice. I noticed plates set on the table, but didn't care to speculate. This time both Melanie and I'd eaten lunch at home. However, we weren't to get off that easily and left at 5:30 p.m. following many good stories, two photo albums, meeting her 88 year old brother whose son is the Dominican Ambassador to England and eating: pigs' feet and cucumbers in a pepper sauce, baked chicken and ham, fried plantain, bread rolls, cake, Jell-O, tea and wine!

I believed I'd never be able to put another thing on the top of my tummy again! Besides being a good cook, Miss Savarin told fascinating stories. One of her photos from 50 years ago was taken on her family's original estate near Clifton, at that time owned by her parents. Miss Savarin's father was an Englishman, her mother a Dominican. Miss Savarin told us she was once in love with a young man who was ten years older than she. But her cousin (ten years younger than she) also loved this same man. "I told him," she said, "but he didn't believe me. Evidently he finally followed up on the idea and found it to be true." To which Miss Savarin's affections shifted, and she gave him over to the younger woman. The fellow did not marry the younger lady until he was old and needed someone to take care of him. "By that time," Miss Savarin said, "he was too old to raise a family, and my cousin spent her married years taking care of an old man!" Miss Savarin feels she got the best of the deal: singlehood, independence, and evidently good health. She keeps her own house, cooks, gardens, and for six days a week runs her shop. Not bad for 80!

For 16 years, before there were roads in Dominica, Miss Savarin taught at the Clifton School while her parents stayed on the Estate so she would have a place to live. She explained how she had her own boatman who she'd notify when she had to make a trip to Portsmouth. And that's how she go to town, by sea. "If I couldn't get hold of my boatman," she said, "I'd walk the five miles to Tanetane on this narrow track (trail) that wasn't even big enough for a bicycle and get a boat at Douglas Bay." When she was 16, after she'd attended a private school, the government asked her to teach at Clifton. "In those days you obeyed order." She said, "But it was okay because I had lots of respect. Many of the students were older than me and bigger. The parents gave their children switches for me to whip them. The children always came to school and they always gave me the switches!"

On the day after Boxing Day, Luke, his wife Bethude, and their two boys, Christan (6) and Terrann (4), took us swimming at Douglas Bay accompanied by fried fish, rum punch, and chocolate candy! Then they brought us home to their apartment for lunch followed by a trip to Cottage for their niece's First Communion celebration. Luke no longer drives a Toyota pick-up, but now drives a small white Toyota Corona: comfy – just like up-town! I promised no more food stories, but believe it or not, Bethude had fixed turkey, pork short ribs, beans, rice (colored red, green and yellow), pea/cabbage/tomato salad, and a yam bake (sliced yams, cheese, butter and milk baked like scallop potatoes). I now know why people leave the island for the holidays: to get away from the food! You know I don't mean that. I enjoyed every bite!

Before Christmas our work days were getting pretty stressful due to a few cultural misunderstandings on our part as well as "theirs." This misunderstanding coupled with the pre-Christmas blues made both Melanie and I ready for a break. Now, it just so happened that on December 30, Barbara Dawson from 49er ROP and her family planned to stop in Martinique (French Island just south of Dominica) while on a holiday cruise in the Caribbean. For those of you who know (and don't know) Barb, she's just what the doctor ordered! Melanie and hopped a plane Wednesday morning, landed in Martinique at 9:00 a.m., took a taxi to the Port, spent a grand and glorious, fun-filled, laughing day with Barb and Jim plus Barb's brothers and sister-in-law from Michigan. We dropped our Peace Corps guise for the day and became tourists complete with a taxi tour, lunch, shopping and hour of talking – all compliments of Barb and family. (Well, Melanie and I did talk a little!) By 5:00 p.m. we were back in Dominica while Barb and family moved slowly out of the Port de Fort de France on their way to St. Maarten.

Flying home across Martinique, the plane darted in and out of greying misty clouds. As the deep gorges of Martinique's volcanic Mont. Pelee came into view below the clouds, I saw my first inverted rainbow! I stared in wonder, and for a mere ten seconds the rainbow became a full circle!

It all sounds so easy, but it's next to impossible for me to concentrate on anything but wok when I'm working. (This doesn't include writing letters home.) Thus, making the decision of whether or not to even go to Martinique, how to go (plane – Liat or boat – Caribbean Express), how long to say)a week, three days, one day), how to get to the airport or port, how much money to take (French and Caribbean) all became insurmountable problems to solve until December 24th. In retrospect, we made all the right decisions except for money. Martinique is EXPENSIVE! We'd only taken 200 francs, and it cost 80 francs just to get from the airport to the port! We'd also taken very little Eastern Caribbean money, and on Wednesday morning after spending the night with PCV Mary in the Carib Territory, we had to pay $30.00 to get to Melville Hall Airport. Once there, we were charged $25.00 Airport Tax to leave the country. Do you remember when I mentioned that I'm an experiential learner? Now, when I want to leave the Island, I'll know the ropes! Oh, yes, we found out on our last of work we had to submit a letter to the ENCORE National Coordinator asking for permission to leave the Island! Also, I learned yesterday that my boss and I, plus the local site manager from Scotts Head Soufriere and a second Peace Corps, will fly to Barbados for two days to meet with the folks from USAID! I'm in the Peace Corps?

PCV Mary who I mentioned above finally got a house! She now lives just a stone's throw from the Atlantic Ocean. Up until a month ago, she was living in a room with a Carib Indian family – one of whom drank heavily, often exasperating Mary! When Melanie and I stayed with her, the night before our Martinique trip, the Atlantic showed us its power and splendor; white foaming, crashing waves. We sat high above the roar, yet still dampened by the spray and awed by the turquoise blue beneath the white foam.

On December 4 (a long time ago!), Melanie and I went to Roseau for our second series of hepatitis shots. We (and Mary) planned to spend the night with PCV Charles in Giraudel because there was a Peace Corps meeting the very next day in Roseau. I think I've mentioned before that riding the transport from Portsmouth to Roseau and back is one of my least favorite things to do! After our shots, grocery shopping, and a bite to eat, we trekked back to the Peace Corps Office to store our groceries for overnight (no sense in carting them to Charles' house), bought lettuce and a watermelon to take to Charles, then headed to the bus stop to catch a ride to Giraudel. Now, Charles had told me the drivers' names and bus colors. I remembered names, but not colors. Arriving at the bus stop, we spotted a green bus almost filled. So as Melanie, Mary and I climbed aboard, I poked my head into the front of the bus and asked, "Are you Eddie, Julian or Griffin?" He said, "I'm Eddie." I said, "We're going to Charles' house." Eddie replied, "I know!" We laughed so hard when we got off the bus at Charles', and I told everyone what Eddie had said. It seems Charles has overnight visitors (other Peace Corps) and they are often grey haired, white ladies! We were quite commonplace to Eddie. It was only in our minds – going to Giraudel for the very first time – that there was any uniqueness. To get to Giraudel, Eddie maneuvered his green transport around the Friday afternoon Roseau traffic onto the road south through New Town's narrow traffic jammed street; then up-up-up the mountainside maneuvering around hairpin curves, descending traffic, narrowing spaces, and in many places, the edge of a cliff!

Traveling an unfamiliar road in Dominica is just like traveling one back home: it takes a lot longer to get there than it will the second time! Coming down the next morning was not near as long nor quite as hairy, but then we saw two rainbows, one double! Giraudel's elevation tops out about 2,000 feet with nothing between it and the Caribbean but lower reaches, greenery, and as the crow flies, about two miles. The transport stopped to let us out a few bends before the main village of Giraudel. In Dominica village houses can be clustered together in a "hollow" or on a hillside, or like Giraudel strung out for a mile or two along one main road. WE found Charles at the end of a short tree canopied lane, graciously awaiting our arrival. Beside smiling faces, we'd also carried food: Macaroni and cheese, fresh baked wheat bread, salad makings, fruitcake, juice, and watermelon! Now, wouldn't any man be happy with that scene? Just imagine a Peace Corps utter joy! Before fixing supper, we watched the sunset from Charles' front porch over crackers and cheese – forgot the wine! It's about 10+ degrees cooler up the mountain. That night the wind blew, and it rained and rained! I put on a long sleeve sweatshirt to keep warm. What a dream that felt like! Needless to say, we all want to go back for another visit.

A side note about Charles – during Peace Corps training he and a PCV from Tennessee, Joyce, became quite enamored after training, even though Joyce went to Grenada for her assignment, the romance continued to bloom. Grenada things didn't go too well for Joyce (a college librarian). And in early November, Joyce went home to Tennessee. Another story that will have to wait its telling for when I get home!

Next, I'd like to share with you some of my journal images that I've written over the past few months. It is now winter here. This means lots of rain, daily rainbows, clouds and shadows, a beautiful softness in the air, the sunlight without its summer harsh ness, and incredible evenings of sounds, sites, and smells (my idea of the threes Ss).

One evening walking home from the beach through the village of Lagoon, the setting sun turned the water a golden hue. Small fishing boats were outlined black against the sky. The river separating Lagoon from Portsmouth ran like liquid gold into the sea! Kenroy, who always escorts us through Lagoon (which has one street) to Portsmouth, calls Lagoon "The Valley of Desolation." He protects us (Melanie mostly) from the "cat calls."

Another day, on our way back to work after lunch, we saw Kenroy who agreed to take us swimming at Douglas Bay. It was beautiful: few people, clouds, sun went down over the Cabrits (two extinct volcanic peaks), mist shrouded Morne AuDiables formed clouds which moved towards us then vanished like puffs of smoke. Kenroy did cartwheels in the sand and back-flips into the sea while two nearby swimmers (a young white girl and local Rastafarian) looked on. When they emerged from the water, the Rasta was stark naked! Young Dominican males are extremely proud of their bodies and keep them in tip-top shape: walking, running, exercising on the beach, swimming, even riding bicycles – mostly done in conjunction with work. The Indian River Tour Guides, of which Kenroy is one, must row their boats up the river when they're on official tours. Many of them lift weights to keep in shape for rowing!

Before work one morning, I sat on the veranda looking toward a cobalt blue sea. White sun-lit boats made their way from the Purple Turtle area south possibly on the way to Roseau. Dark grey clouds hung over the hills and mountains to the east. Now and again they'd part, letting the sunshine come through or send off a rain cloud followed by a rainbow. A brisk breeze promised a "cool" day. There's an excitement in the air with sunshine versus the suddenness of a heavy laden sky, everything sparkles -- all the varied colors, the green and the sea!

One Saturday on the way to market, as I walked on the road by the Catholic Church that I take each day to work. I thought about the rutted road lined on one side with a stone wall, vehicles moving by, villagers on their way to market and wondered, "Is this what I thought an underdeveloped country was like?" Actually, I never thought about things like that. What I did worry about before I got here seemed to take care of itself. Adjusting is a marvelous thing!

Enough images. I know I've got to tell you more about work or you won't believe I do! But I do – sometimes from 8:30 a.m. to 6:30 p.m.! Melanie and I've come to the conclusion that if we think we've got it figured out – we don't. A student from the local "off shore" medical school came by the ENCORE office one day. He wanted to volunteer to help! We couldn't put him anywhere because everything we do is for the first time. We never know how a task/assignment/project is going to turn out or even if it's going to turn out! From my perspective (even though I still try to control a lot), its all done on faith! Flexibility is a marvelous thing!

We've developed an ENCORE flyer, helped organize the Indian River Tour Guides, met with local groups to tell them about ENCORE, and in late January and February we'll be putting on an environmental education program (still to be developed by us) for the local school children. We organize and attend lots of meetings. (guess who takes the minutes?) A local fishermen's group was the first group to submit an ENCORE project proposal. It's for training in environmentally sound/modern fishing techniques. It must be approved by the Local Site Management Team then forwarded to the National ENCORE Coordinator and National Coordinating Committee for final approval. This process makes ROP and the community college systems look like peaches and cream! Serves me right for ever complaining. Other projects waiting in the wings include a small children's park, beach cleanups/landscaping, trail rehabilitation, local crafts training, and tour guide training.

I get tired. I get discouraged. And as a few of you found out before Christmas, I get sad and miss you all! But for the most part Dominica is a pretty special place as are its people. In fact, it's pretty much like home. Thank you so much for the holiday mail, wishes and presents. After receiving so much I felt the usual guilt pangs, but everything is back to normal today.

With love, Mary Ann

January 9, 1993

P.S. Yesterday PCV Mary called and she'd spent two day since the Roseau hospital after an apparent heart attack. On the 10th she flew to Washington, D.C. for test. The PC medical officer feels her "attack" was stress related and not a heart attack, but there's no equipment in the Eastern Caribbean for testing. I've had no news since the 9th, but I'm hoping she's okay.

Mom and Bill will be "Caribbean cruising" to Dominica on February 17, 1993. Such an exciting thing for me (and them) to look forward to.

January 16, 1993

As you can see it takes me a long time to get the start of a letter to the finished product! I found out yesterday that I won't be going to Barbados! Another interesting story reserved for coming home. I am in the Peace Corps!

GOAT WATER (Stew)
From "The Art of Caribbean Cooking
By Yolande Cools-Lartigue

"(This is a dish for serving many in a casual way! It is very good for all-day entertainment and is allowed to simmer on very low heat continuously. You may add ingredients to increase as the day goes on. It is actually eaten in almost soup form, or rather like an extended stew with lots of good gravy.)

| ½ goat carcass | 1 head garlic |
| 6 large onions | 1 hot green pepper |

1 head celery	3 Tbsp. vinegar
6 carrots	1 sprig thyme
3 turnips or 6 parsnips	3 Tbsp. salt
1 doz. eddoes or tannias (root plants)	½ cup oil

"Method: Cut up goat into fairly small pieces and put in a large container. Peel and crush garlic and add to goat. Add salt, finely chopped hot pepper, chopped thyme, vinegar, and about 2 cups cold water. Mix well and allow to stand for about two hours. In a large skillet, pour oil and place over heat. When oil is very hot, add goat, reserving any liquid. Sauté, stirring often until lightly browned. Then add liquid from marinade and enough water to cover. Cook until tender. Lower heat and allow to simmer gently for several hours before serving so that goat and vegetables are soft. Keep on very low heat and serve as required. You may add vegetables and seasonings to increase quantity as the day goes on." Yummy!!!

January 31, 1993

Dear Mom and Dad:

Happy Anniversary! Happy Valentine's Day, too!! Well, your trip is getting closer and by the time you get this – even closer! Hope you are able to stay bus so as not to get too anxious. According to Barbara Dawson on the boat your every wish will be taken care of. And if the Indian River Tour Guides are an example of how you'll be taken care of on shore, you have not a worry in the world. Easier said than done. Right? But I know all will go well for you. Mom will probably enjoy all the deck chairs and fresh air, reading books while Bill takes in every activity on the boat. I've taken your wishes to heart and am planning very little for your time on Dominica. I've been in touch with Caroline and given her a list of things for you to bring. I appreciate that very much. Thank you in advance. I received your itinerary. I never thought you'd be going to all those places. Lowell once received a "deal" through Auburn Travel to go to Cancun – seven days and seven night's thing! He had to buy all of his meals (and keep in mind liquor) and it almost broke him. You've probably already asked Auburn Travel what's included in your package and what's not. If you haven't, I'd do that: meals, tips, activities on ship, tours on land, et cetera, et cetera. If they "hem and haw," pin them down!

Still no sign of the November general letter or tape. They must have gone the way of the winds! I have both a January 10 and January 14 letter from you here now. I bet the snow on the mountain is beautiful. Hope Dr. Alan is enjoying it. Caroline said Saturday (30) was a gorgeous day! That is nice of Carol to have you down before your flight to take you to the airport. I got a nice letter from her and will write back soon. Glad you enjoyed the tape. Sounds like Doug and Janie had a good trip. I pronounce Roseau: Rozo, Roezo, and Roseoh. Glad, too, Bill feels okay with "upcoming" operation. That did worry me that it was being put off. But I understand better now after talking to Caroline.

Thank you, too, Bill, for the personal note.
See you soon. Love Mary Ann

February 17, 1993

Dear Mom and Bill:

Thank you for letting me keep the photos. I looked at them at least four times! Melanie also enjoyed. When you sent them back to Janie be sure to tell her that I've seen them because on her envelope she says she'll send them to me.

It was so special having you and Bill visit. And like I kept saying, the best thing was that the cruise is going so, so well! I've heard all my life (well almost) how fun cruises are. It was interesting to see all the people and so many younger. The ships that come into Portsmouth seem to carry much older tourists.

Alick, our driver, seemed to feel you had a very good time. And in the true Dominican way, that made him very happy. Hope the rest of your cruise was as successful as the beginning. We really didn't fit very much into our five hours, but it is good not to be rushed. I'm so sorry you felt rushed at lunch. I wondered if the noise level contributed to a feeling of not being relaxed. Next time we'll go to a closed-in restaurant.

I forgot to tell you that our friends in Portsmouth said to say hello – especially Kenroy. He is the young fellow singing at the beginning of the Xmas tape. I've wanted to show Dominica to someone from home since I first arrived. So at least I've now shown one small part. It was fun. I also enjoyed going on the ship. I think it would be fun to have your staterooms and sleep easily at night after a day of site seeing and all.

Barb's clothes are perfect – I'll tell her so. Thank you, too, for the tape and books and lovely yellow blossoms! Caroline did good, too. I'll tell her, also.

Welcome home! Where to next?

Love Mary Ann

March 13, 1993

Dear Family and Friends:

Having just returned from a five-day Peace Corps workshop on environmental education at the "Fancy" Layou River Hotel, I'm recovering from "Reverse Cultural Shock": White folks, hot water, swimming pools, bathtubs, food fixed by other hands, no laundry, and, miracle of miracles, planned activities actually taking place, and more or less on time,

"Fancy' is set off to qualify the hotel. Set in the lush Layou River valley – surrounded by towering cliffs that support every shade of green and plant texture imaginable, sunlight (and full moon)

highlighting first one green then another white water rushing by on its way to the sea – the Layou River Hotel is all that is on its way to the sea – the Layou River hotel is all that is Dominica! Half our shower rod fell the first night barely missing Mary Peterson's head! The other half hung all week from the wall by the threads of one screw. Water seeped through our wall on its way from a leak in room 30! The first day we had two towels, two wash cloths, a bath mat, and two hand towels. After that I felt lucky to have two bath towels. See how quickly I can turn into complainer? On the third day, I stood at the end of the bathtub once again to fix the shower rod and all the tile between the tub and wall collapsed into a dark hole! You should have seen me when I took my first shower! I was like a kid with a new bicycle. I stood there in the hot water and giggled and giggled, at the same time feeling guilty as heck because I let it wash over me and over me. I've not felt like that very often in my life! It was a most marvelous sensation; not the guilt, the feeling of that hot water!

In attending the workshop, which was for all Peace Corps Environmental Ed Teachers and ENCORE PCVs in the Eastern Caribbean and their local counterparts, I missed the entrance into Portsmouth of the Duke of Edinburgh and the Royal Yacht. Not that I was anxious to see Prince Phillip, but after he was welcomed by the Prime Minister his motorcade crept down the main street of Portsmouth preceded by a royal guard past hundreds of uniformed school children standing at attention!

So much has happened since I last wrote. But as important as the events all seemed when they occurred, most thoughts and feelings have faded away or taken a back seat to newer memories. To catch you up then I must rely on my journal. My apologies if I've already sent a few of these stories home.

Here in Dominica when something happens, the phenomenon may take on a name totally unrelated to the real occurrence. Such is the case of the winter's flu outbreak, locally referred as Courts. Named after the first of its kind department store to open on the Island, Courts is ushered in by a sore throat and headache followed closely by a cough, sinus infection, aches and pains, maybe a fever, and more often than not, eyes that no longer sparkle! Sound familiar?

Somehow the nicknaming tends to take the seriousness out of a situation; and as with so many happenings in the Caribbean, it is then taken lightly! Courts did not spare me, but I seemed to get rid of it easily. Unlike the locals, I rested – literally went to bed for a day after drinking chicken noodle soup for breakfast. The next day, friend Luke brought me a local bush tea remedy accompanied by Vic's Vapor-Rub and camphor oil.

Going to bed is not considered a local remedy for any type of illness. It seems that only happens if you're taken to the hospital in Roseau. Even our eight-year-old friend, Loic, "jumped-up" at Carnival time under the influence of Courts: The theory being, "If you stop, the illness will really get you down!" Last August, friend Kenroy, didn't stop and that time his "flu" turned into pneumonia which landed him in Roseau's Princess Margaret Hospital flat on his back!

Carnival has come and gone (February 22 and 23), but evidently with much less turmoil than in the past. Turmoil may not be the proper descriptive noun to use. Each year it seems many young ones are born nine months after Carnival. Having now "experienced" Carnival, I could venture that the babies are due, in part, to the phenomenon known as "jump-up" where males and females of all ages follow a band, or a truck carrying a Hi-Fi blaring a lively tune. The "jump-up" dance step is best described as a sensuous, hip-moving two-step motion that carries the "Jumper-Uppers" down the street in time to the music! Quite a sight and quite a sound. The human parade converged on the streets of Portsmouth from 10:00 a.m. till 10:00 p.m. on both the 22nd and 23rd.

During Carnival Melanie had company from the States, Chris – a polite young man from Virginia who also had a good sense of humor. Even he couldn't keep up the pace! Polly Zimpel, PCV who lives in Trafalgar, spent the two days with me. We watched "Jump-Up" while seated on the steps of Miss Bess' craft shop while she told us all about the carnivals of other times when they wore masks and elaborate costumes, and how the vanilla bean was TOPS before the banana. Vanilla lost out when producers or shippers began putting in false vanilla beans – there went the vanilla bean market!

This next story is for all of you, but pay even closer attention if you have ties with a local Methodist Church. Two groups of volunteers from Wisconsin came to Zicack to help the local Methodist Church build a community hall. The local church knew for months that the volunteers were coming! But nothing much progressed. It seems funds (also sent by the same Wisconsin group to Dominica) never got out of the Church's hierarchy in discouraged but enjoyed their two weeks on Dominica anyway. On their last night they invited Melanie and I to visit with them. But since it was Carnival, Melanie and Chris went to "Jump-Up" while Polly and I visited the Methodists. The first group so liked our insight, they left a note for the second group to contact us right away.

When the second group arrived, again 12, they had me over for dinner – Melanie had Courts! Such nice people, some retired, many teachers and nurses, mostly husbands and wives. One couple is seriously thinking about Peace Corps when they retire. We felt their frustration – only having two weeks and wanting to do so much. Anyway, the Wisconsin group has given all it can and asked us to spread the word. If there is a church out there that would be interested in sending volunteers, please contact: Reverend Joyce Rohan, c/o Portsmouth Methodist Church, Portsmouth, Commonwealth of Dominica, and West Indies. Telephone number is 1-809-445-5990.

Speaking of giving to a "worthy" cause. Remember my trip to Martinique at Christmastime? At that time I shared my wardrobe sorrows with Barb Dawson. I'm now the best dressed woman in Dominica! Lest you think my Mom and Bill's visit via a Caribbean cruise has been replaced by other memories: they carried Barb's hand-me-downs! Just joking, of course. But both very special. It was incredible to drive up alongside this huge glaringly white cruise ship in the Roseau harbor and see two people out of a thousand that I knew! Along with clothes, hugs and news of home, I got a tour of their cruise ship, the Festivale. Seeing Mom and Bill was like they'd just dropped in for a Sunday afternoon visit at home. To me, absolutely no connection had been lost. It was a secure comfortable feeling. Not until the ride home to Portsmouth after they sailed did I have any kind of reaction, and it was a totally unexpected one and new to me. I got quite confused, sad, and a little angry because I wanted some of the luxury and pampering I'd seen on the boat! Strange way for homesickness to surface!

The weather has changed. February was known as umbrella and sunglass weather. It is now the dry season; sun, strong winds, leaves turn and fall on deciduous trees, the sky gets so blue, so does the sea. Rain may come once every two weeks or it may not, grasses brown and die. It is dusty!

I've gone through one more transition in my life as a Peace Corps volunteer. Hopefully the next corner won't carry such extreme highs and low lows. Those of you at home who buffered and helped this last evolution – thank you! For the rest of you, I'll try to explain.

First of all, one day in early February, on my way to spend a weekend at Mary Peterson's in the Carib Territory, walking through Roseau to catch a transport to the other side of the Island, day pack on my back, camera slung over my shoulder, dressed in a skirt, blouse and tennis shoes, it came to me that this is now my life. I am in the Peace Corps; and before I left Auburn, somewhere deep down inside I'd visualized this scene. This was how it was supposed to be. I think at that moment I felt younger than I had felt since leaving California. Also, a sense of well-being came over me that I would make it; that it wasn't all peaches and cream. I was in the middle of a developing country and so, so much was different than home. I now know that – it had sunk in and maybe from then on I wouldn't get thrown quite so far! But besides all that revelation, it seemed ENCORE had a life of its own. I'm not sure yet if it's the personalities, the bureaucracy, the fact it's a USAID project, or a combination of all three. But in February all I wanted to do was divorce myself from ENCORE's intrigue and just get on with it.

At this point none of that seems possible. But the Peace Corps has proposed that for PC ENCORE volunteers there be a project written for us within the bigger ENCORE project – otherwise there seems to be no way of evaluating our progress or the reaching of any goals. Melanie and I heartily agree! Plus, I know I didn't join the Peace Corps to be a secretary! It's funny, too, how my perspective evolves over time. A little like the more you know, the less you wish you knew! Besides the intrigue, as Melanie says, everything (ENCORE related) seems suspect, gossip abounds, and it's hard to separate the white lies from the lies told for a purpose. I'm not sure any of this makes sense (actually, I'm sure it doesn't), but the stories for telling at home are growing.

In my last letter I mentioned PCV Mary Peterson had been sent to Washington, D.C., for medical tests. She is fine and back working diligently setting up the Life Lab Program (science through a school garden) at the Territory's Primary School. When I spent the weekend with her, it was just like camping; water carried from the cistern, meals eaten outside, dishes washed on a wooden counter, potty in the outhouse. The outhouse overlooks a banana garden and the Atlantic Ocean quite an experience! Sunday, we cooked up yummy meals (still one of my favorite things to do), sharing food and drink with a young lady from Canada assigned to the Carib Territory for a Community Development Internship as part of her Canadian University's course of study. The three of us (between meals) soaked in salt pools (actually tide pools) at the ocean's edge and showered under a pipe that captured its icy water from a canyon stream. The salt pools, as they are called locally, are naturally hollowed out on a long, wide rocky bench about eye level with the Atlantic's crashing waves. As we soaked, an occasional wave crashed high enough to spread chilling foamy sea water across the rocky bench, thus refilling the pools with fresh salt water. None of the tide pool creatures paid us a heed!

At 5:30 Monday morning, I caught a Seventh Day Adventist School transport back to Zicack, walking into my front door at 7:10 a.m. I highly recommend Mary's place for a weekend getaway. In fact, any company I might have has an open invitation.

Man of you still write and ask, "What do you do? I'm still unclear." Maybe by my next letter I'll have a clearer picture for you other than all the secretarial/organizing/project administration type duties. The whole evolving of the ENCORE project has been one of incredible frustration for both Melanie and myself. We are trying to break away (slowly) from the paperwork mill and begin work on a project of our own with a community group.

The Environmental Education program we developed and presented reached approximately 600 students in four schools. It became tiring by the last week, but it was very rewarding and fun. The students and their teachers enjoyed our posters (we used lots of pictures cut out of my Audubon and Sierra Club magazines) as well as the way we involved the students in each classroom presentation.

Our next big project is a Grand March for the Environment on April 22 (Earth Day). The march has been selected as ENCORE's Regional Earth Day event which means dignitaries, T.V. ENCORE personnel from St. Lucia, even and ENCORE song competition. So whatever "project within a project" surfaces, it won't happen until after Earth Day! Do you think we can out-do the Duke!

I think of you all so often. I love your letters/cards and calls. Your support is really quite incredible.

With much love, Mary Ann

April 12, 1993

Dear Family and Friends:

It's Easter Monday on Dominica. The west wind's blowing, softening just a little the heat of the past week. Besides bringing a coolness through our window, the breeze lifts a white kite with a long red tail higher and higher over Portsmouth. Happy Easter!

Today is the last day of a four-day holiday: one I'm so saddened to say brought tragedy to this small island and to all of us Eastern Caribbean Peace Corps. Joyce, the lovely PCV lady from Tennessee who had been assigned to Grenada and subsequently sent back home, drowned here on Good Friday.

As you might remember, she and Charles (Dominican Peace Corps) fell in love last July during Peace Corps training. The romance flourished from that point, and when Joyce was separated (a Peace Corps term for being sent home), she made plans to come back and visit Charles over Easter vacation. This past week, while Joyce was here, they rented a car and traveled on Thursday to Mary Peterson's in the Carib Territory where they spent the night. The next morning they planned to come to Portsmouth. But first they and Mary piled in the car and the three of them headed south to L'Esclier Tete-chien ("the Steps"), a crack in the Earth's surface where eons ago lava intruded forming a long staircase from the mountain to the sea. "The Steps" actually go far down into the ocean. Before Joyce drowned, I wanted to visit the spot at minus tide. I no longer care to see L'Esclier Tete-chien! Friday was Mary's first trip. Charles had been twice before.

When I talked to Mary she said, "Charles and Joyce had just brought me their cameras because they were starting to get splashed. They were about 15 feet below me and further out. We were all on a high area above the sea; they were at the edge. Out of nowhere a wave came from the right. When the foam cleared, they were not there!" I can only just begin to imagine Mary's terror and her screams at that point. They continued, she told me, until she saw both Charles and Joyce below in the churning water, watched Charles swim across to where he climbed out, and realized Joyce had not followed. Mary feels the wave or rocks stunned Joyce, also when Charles told her in the water to follow him, she became disoriented. I think Joyce was about 45. She was a strong, strong swimmer and a runner. Her body's not yet been found. Mary and Charles are doing "okay." My feelings range from complete disbelief to hatred of the Atlantic, something you all know I'd come to Love!

Just a side note of no consequence: I spent last weekend with Mary again. We only watched the sea and waves that day and did not go down near the tide pools by her house because the waves were so powerful. But because I had been the last the villagers had seen visiting Mary, they thought the lady from Portsmouth had been swept out to sea. I keep saying how the island is one of complete contrast. Again, that's been brought home: Balmy breezes and a nightmare. What often seems the hardest to believe is a story like this next one:

April 11, 1993

Dear Charles:

For a number of reasons I want to write to you about how I feel. Besides still not believing it all, I got angry at the Atlantic Ocean. You and Joyce being swept off into the sea seems so instant and so foreign to me. At home, we are awake, constantly, of the ability of the vehicle to instantly take a life. But the sea's ability to do the same is only read about. At least in my reality. From the time I was a young girl I have been awe of it – its power, beauty and unpredictability. Mary and I had sat for 2 ½ hours just last Sunday mesmerized by all of that!

I've just come home from Easter Sunday Catholic Church where resurrection after death took precedence over all. I've tried to read into Joyce's death, taking place on Good Friday, a significance of death and being reborn. I also struggle with her seemly unwelcome reception in the Caribbean first – being separated from Peace Corps and then to actually tragically die here!

But, Charles, throughout my life I've also become somewhat of a fatalist – believing often that things are meant to be. And maybe it was Joyce's turn no matter where she might have been or no matter if she'd ever been sent to the Caribbean for Peace Corps or not. But she was and because of that she received the blessing of meeting and knowing you. Knowing you as I do, I feel you will be able to look at it that way and realize what a gift she gave you and what a gift you gave her.

Last Thursday we heard a young white man was looking all over Portsmouth for Melanie. It turns out, when she finally met him, he's wind-surfing his way from island to island. When he reached Dominica on Wednesday, he'd just come from Martinique, before that St. Lucia, St. Vincent, and Grenada. That means hours on this little board across vast expanses of sea. He wears a wetsuit, carries small navigational instruments and that's about it. No room for much more, not even shoes. He'd gotten Melanie's name from a St. Vincent Peace Corps he'd met up with down there. You explain it. I can't. The kite's still flying!

During the Easter Week and celebration, church services could be had any day of the week. Since I'm trying to be faithful to the Catholic Church with a little deviation now and again to the Methodist Church, there's been plenty for me to do: Holy Thursday Mass, Good Friday Meditation and Service, and Easter Sunday Mass and Celebration. I missed Saturday night – heard it went from 11:00 p.m. to 2:00 a.m.! Every time I enter the Portsmouth Catholic Church, I anticipate beauty and drama. I've yet to be disappointed.

On Easter Sunday, for example, amid oppressive heat (at 8:00 a.m. in the morning), extra chairs in the aisle and still people standing, voices lift the soul, the sweat pours down my face forgotten – blended with tears for the outpouring of love these people offer "The Father, Son and Holy Spirit." Sunday the young people acted out Christ's rising and discovery of the empty tomb. The dancers all wore white robes with red headpieces against their dark, dark skins. A lone female singer's voice rang out with such clarity throughout the church. Everywhere else on Easter Day that I went, similar sounds could be heard, if not for real, from blaring radios and cassettes turned to peak volume.

The grinding ENCORE/Peace Corps wheel still turns. On April 26-30 we're due to attend another Peace Corps training: This one on St. Lucia for Project Development. But the Head/Encore "Powers that be" won't let boss Thomas Paul go with us. So whatever "project" Melanie and work on won't get Mr. Paul's input or blessings.

At work, besides helping write and ultimately type (computer), eight community project proposals applying for the "local site" share of ENCORE funds, we've been slowly putting the April 22 Earth Day Parade together. The parade or Grand March as it's called here, began as an idea from our friend Luke Azielle. Luke's also involved in ENCORE. It's now, as I mentioned in my last letter, become the regional ENCORE celebration for Earth Day. But as such a lot of the "expectations" have been taken out of our hands. Speakers have grown in number to include the Parliamentary Representative, Minister of Education and Minister of Agriculture.

Our original list of local speakers has receded to a position of introductory remarks! So much is out of our control, yet the school children must still stand in the hot sun and listen, we can't do with a hitch? Not in a long, long time. But then if it did, that would not be the Dominican way!

ENCORE's struggle seems more and more one of control. And speaking of such, I keep wanting to get out from under Mr. Paul's control! Besides being a naturally dominating Dominican male (hope I don't offend anyone), Thomas has almost entirely regulated us to office work while he "develops" new projects. I sincerely believe he does this unconsciously, but also because, being independent thinking women, we often disagree with him – a "no-no" in public. My latest thinking is ENCORE's "got-a-be" ENCORE whether I'm here or not. So maybe I'll move to a new village and commute to work. In the new village, at least, I'll be out from under. Probably wishful thinking. I hope not. My only dilemma seems to be to find a village where I can get a Sunday ride to Father "Reggie's" church!

Let me back up for a while and see if I can give you a few memories and images from my journal.

I almost forgot. I had a birthday and am now a tanned, ten pounds heavier, 58-year-old. The cards and calls from home were just great. Thank you! Luke took Melanie and me for a moonlight ride to Calibishie for a birthday drink. Melanie got car sick coming home and I was in the back seat. Kenroy left a lovely mint green and violet vase (with cloth flowers) wrapped in shiny bright red paper topped by a pink bow sitting on the veranda. Then he got worried Melanie would be jealous because it was prettier than her birthday present!

One day I enjoyed my 75-plus year old neighbor's confession of love on a seemingly deserted street on my way to Saturday market only to hear these words coming from behind the shrubbery as I passed by, "Oh! Papa! Oh! Papa!" Norris, the confessor, is a dear sweet man, about five feet tall, who carries a small cassette player/radio with him wherever he goes, whether to church or "down the hill" first thing every morning. The only conclusion I've drawn about the early morning walks is to use the bathroom. There's the bay, but in Portsmouth there's also a public convenience (a public toilet and shower). Norris and his wife live across the street in a small wooden "house."

Another day, when I stopped by Eunella's shop to look for sunscreen and explained that the doctor said I had capillary damage on my face she said, "But I find it looking so good on you!" Life does have its upside. And I hope you all know I'm joking.

This past Saturday, Melanie and I traveled to Vieille Case, a trip we'd promised ourselves for at least eight months. And such a trip it turned out to be! Most days buses come down from Vieille Case in the morning and go back up in the afternoon. But a friend felt if we went to market on Saturday we could find a ride up with a vendor; and because it was the day before Easter, getting a transport down later in the afternoon would not be a problem. He was right.

You should have seen us! Sitting in the back of a pickup with 11 other women on built-in side seats under a roof-canopy loaded with sacks of provisions, fruit, flour and all else these Pennville ladies needed to purchase on their one day in town! Vieille Case is on the Atlantic side of Dominica, northeast of Portsmouth; Pennville is three miles north of Vieille Case. Besides our 13 crammed bodies, the pickup bed carries fish, eggs, filled baskets and bags, propane tanks, packages, anything considered too delicate to ride "atop."

After innumerable stops throughout Portsmouth and at least three trips around the town (important not to forget anyone), the little pickup headed to Vieille Case, swaying and leaning at every corner and groaning up every hill! There are corners and there are hills! At one point we were riding along the cliff high above the Atlantic! I remember when this used to scare me!

We crawled out in the middle of Vieille Case, I crawled – Melanie walked, only to be greeted by a prominent local citizen who escorted us through the Catholic cemetery to overlook the ocean and back to his house for grapefruit juice. This same fellow met us again for a soda in a small, almost hidden, concrete shop. Fun. Fun. Fun! And cool! The first mass ever held on Dominica was held in Vieille Case in the 1600s in the tent-like hut of a Carib Indian

Not only is there history in Vieille Case, it's the cleanest village on the island, houses stand further apart from one another than in most villages, and miracle of miracles, there are trees with grass under them for relaxing in the shade! We're going back.

In February my good friend and returned Peace Corps volunteer, Bob Morelli, from Oroville, met with a severe accident; a drunken driver, traveling 55 miles an hour knocked Bob and his backpack about 20 feet into the middle of the road. Bob, who planned to retire soon and hike a portion of the Pacific Crest Trail, was resting and watching the sunset on his way home from work when he was hit. Walking back and forth to work carrying a loaded pack was Bob's way of getting in shape for his hike. This very special gentleman is going to be laid up for quite a while – knowing Bob, not as long as the doctors think! Now his name, along with his courageous wife Patty is spoken often in the Portsmouth Catholic church!

Before closing this letter, I'll share another recipe, one I'm cooking tonight. Take care of each one of you. You might not know how special you are but I do!

Love, Mary Ann
P.S. The kite stayed aloft for the whole afternoon!

April 13; 9:00 p.m.

I did call Charles this evening and I did tell him all the things I said in the letter. He told me he got a card from her (Joyce) today and all it said was, "Hi! I love you." I think that is so very beautiful, like a gift from the Heaven. Last night Kentie came by and told us of the "whirlpools" or jets as he called them and blow holes and tunnels under the sea. Today Thomas told us about the geology of the eastern side of Dominica (Lava and lobs and the Atlantic and both the Guadalupe Channel and Martinique Channel are narrow and here little ole Dominica getting the brunt of it all! Mary's friend Norma is here from Wichita, Kansas, JoAnn's last day in Portsmouth was today. She goes home tomorrow. She is a talker! Mary was glad to hear about the underwater blowholes; it made sense to her that maybe Joyce got twisted around rather than stunned. Mary images today: a drunk man walking down middle of the street playing the harmonica and singing and staggering – played a good harmonica. Cleetis' kids (two) still alone. Not sure when Cleetis comes home. Gutzy little kids. Key walked over and back. This morning they went all alone to take their showers – the little boy stark naked! He stands often on front porch, one thumb in his mouth and one hand on his penis. A beautiful study!

I'm feeling more and more like ENCORE's not going to be what it's cracked up to be. Keep trying to think of Polly's words – "accept things as they are and not like you'd want them to be."

April 14; 8:30 p.m.

Staff meeting in Roseau today. All the way in to town! A complete feeling of not being needed. That ENCORE and Dominica can do without me completely. Roti for lunch at a new place. Picked up chairs at Astophans, made hair appointment for Saturday. Will go to tomorrow for Joyce's service. Reading more and more of woman and Wobles – good, good; and maybe healing possible. Called Mrs. Valerie tonight re: proposal not being okay. She goes Tuesdays to Toucoure for lessons maybe next week I'll go! Cleeties finally home! Little boy laid down on steps and fell fast asleep this afternoon. Head on top larger step and feet and legs hanging over. Dry, dry all over island's west side. Saw bush fire in Espanola area. Sky for days has been same here as sea. Mary stories about danger of Atlantic between Castle Bruce and Margot Bad. This a.m. realized how sad Zicack and Portsmouth people would be if I moved. Maybe can do both. Or I need to get involved in project here other than ENCORE. I like Roseau today. Saw Polly alongside the road waiting for Mary and Norma. Felt anger today over Melanie "playing: with Rennie. Feel maybe I need to talk to Ophelia if I have problems because Thomas is so macho. I told him today that Mrs. Green said keys only for me. Images yesterday – old man, staggering down street, playing harmonica and jabbering!

April 19, 1993

Grand March Thursday: Today Monday, three days before: Police in Roseau say we sent letter to wrong person – they had to have big meeting to make decision if they could have it still;

May 16, 1993; 11:30 a.m. Sunday

Dear Mom and Bill:

As they say in the Eastern Caribbean, "Long time since I've written you!" Thanks for sending the copy of my latest newsletter. Given all the going and comings there, it was doubly nice you got it off in the mail. I sincerely hope things have settled down into somewhat of your "normal" routine. Glad Bill is out of the woods, so to speak. You both must have had some anxious moments. I appreciate hearing of your experience first-hand. Others have kept me posted, but it's not quite the same thing.

You've probably heard my good news – Lori, Kyle, Josh and Caroline are coming to visit. How could I be so lucky?

I do know that since your letter Bill had to go back in the hospital – but the outcome was expected to be a good one. That's great! Isn't it amazing how hospital stays/surgery, sickness can completely take over your life? Good luck, Bill, with the bladder control.

Let's see if I can catch you up on some of the happenings here: Melanie and I went to St. Lucia for a week of Peace Corps training in small project development. It was the best to date!

The trainer was a Dominican woman, Lucia Blaize who promises to give us any needed support for our ENCORE work. It, the week, was also a great get-away as we stayed in a nice guesthouse – had all our meals fixed for us and enjoyed seeing old Peace Corps that we'd trained with last July. Can you believe that?

My Catholic Church education continues via a nine-week pilgrimage to Toucare (a fishing village north of Portsmouth) where I take part in a Novena to St. Anthony in the village's small wooden Catholic Church every Tuesday evening. All will culminate in the Feast of St. Anthony on June 13th. Then yesterday I traveled to Roseau to take part in one day of a three-day Charismatic Renewal Conference: workshop speakers, "renewal empowerment," saving and all! Quite an experience, one I'm not sure I enjoyed, but one I'm glad I didn't miss. Just like the Women's Mission I took part in here in Portsmouth where I was the only white woman among 500 Dominicans – I think yesterday I stood out among about 1,000 black people. So many villages are isolated, and yet the whole island is like one big small town where everyone knows about everyone else!

I had fun writing as usual because Thomas Paul is off training in St. Lucia for two weeks so Melanie and I are enjoying the rest from his high energy! He was unable to go to St. Lucia when we did because this training had been scheduled for him way in advance. In a way, I'm thankful for that.

Well, today has been one of laundry, window washing, sweeping the floor, sleeping in, cooking beans and rice, washing my hair and now letter writing. Amazing what I can get done if I stay home from church!

Love you, Mary Ann

May 19, 1993

Dear Family and Friends:

Mr. Paul is training on St. Lucia! Two blessed weeks on our own! But in all fairness and honesty, it will be good to have him back, I think. At this point, we aren't quite sure how we'll deal with his exuberance after our relaxing two weeks. But we should be more or less fortified for a few days at least.

May is supposedly the hottest month on the island. Even the locals are affected. The streets are empty in early afternoons, small shops close, people ask, "How is the heat treating you?" I wrote home to Lori yesterday that I believed if I stood in the middle of the road long enough I'd come out roasted like a chicken who'd been left in the oven for an hour, only not as moist. All that moisture would be "sweated" out of me.

To wrap up a few things I'd mentioned in my last letter – Joyce's body was recovered in waters off of Guadalupe, an island just north of Dominica, on the Monday following her drowning. Positive identification, however, wasn't made for almost two weeks, because they had to fly her dental records in from Washington, D.C. The body had traveled many miles in such a short time. Locals say that proves how really strong the currents are. Mr. Paul told us that persons who have drowned on the Atlantic side of the island often get into the channel between Dominica and Guadalupe and end up in South America! Evidently, it was unusual that her body made it across the channel.

The inquest was held just this past week. Charles told his story, but Mary did not have to testify, nor would they let her listen to what Charles described just in case they needed to hear her story. She just sat in the hall all day! As you can imagine, Joyce's drowning affected many, many people besides we Dominican Peace Corps volunteers. Locals, who I just slightly know, still approach me on the street and say how sorry they are. Thank you at home for your words of sympathy.

The Earth Day Grand March and Rally as many of you already know, was a success! By the end of the day, DBS (Roseau radio station) had taped the whole event including the four young song competitors, television cameras had filmed it all, and suddenly, ENCORE Portsmouth was famous all over the island.

Before the big day arrived, the head ENCORE office in St. Lucia decided we could make it just a local thing after all! No one even came from St. Lucia! I think this spurred a lot of the local people on to make it even better than we'd first planned.

On the actual day, my three jobs were to first organize the parade and head everyone in the right direction. This worked beautifully because the teachers, principals and students are used to this sort of thing, they do it like clockwork; everyone showed up; and Melanie, Kenroy and Mr. Mills organized the posters. Have you ever tried to staple poster paper to a hard stick with a broken staple gun? Or figure out how to keep everything from flying off when a big gust of wind comes busting by?

My second task was to give credit to the schools, thank them for their efforts and hand out plaques. As each principal came on stage to accept the plaque, I shook their hand and a photographer took our picture. This was fun, because I'm basically a "ham" at heart and love the limelight! But the funniest thing was that morning I'd decided to wear a straw hat that I'd just purchased the week before in Roseau, and in all the photos I looked just like a tourist with this little straw hat sitting on top of my head!

My next duty consisted of organizing a small (50-person) reception following the Rally. This would have worked fine, but the food never came! Well, actually the food did come about an hour late which turned out to be a good thing because lots of the people got tired of waiting and left. So we ended up with just enough food for the people who persevered! Ophelia didn't come because that would have made the day perfect! "And we can't have that!" On Friday morning she called us at home to say we were a success! "Very professionally done," was the compliment she was the proudest about. I agreed!

Just so you won't think everything WAS perfect, this is what I wrote in my journal on April 19th. "Grand March Thursday, today Monday – three days to go – police in Roseau say we sent letter to wrong person. Now they have to have a big meeting to make a decision to see if we can still hold parade and rally. Baldwin can't lead prayer – I asked Murphy, Mrs. Andre, and Father Reggie! All said no! City Council doesn't know about parade and all. Thomas Paul even went to city council meeting last week. We'd also written a letter – wonder where it went? Program turned out good. Thomas is now getting his cousin to play the guitar, not Felix in Educational Office who I'd already asked. Haven't any idea if and when invitations went out and to whom! Over the weekend under a lot of stress! Today better because so much to do."

Yesterday Melanie talked of building self-confidence. Each day we force ourselves into a new situation – thinking, ideas, and often values different than our own, meet new people, and iron out new problems. When there is something that we want or have to do, we gulp and jump in saying, "Well, I did such and such yesterday here I go again!"

Since I revealed to you in my last letter about my neighbor's declaration of love, I've received a second whisper of adoration. This time on the main street of Portsmouth at high noon! Kenroy once told me that if someone is this daring in the sunlight, "Watch out after dark!" But I think he is talking about the young fellows, not the ones who tell me, "I love you!"

Just a note about the Small Project Development training on St. Lucia at the end of April. It was great! Our trainer was a Dominican lady with an incredible sense of humor who works with rural development projects. She took her shoes off while presenting, involved us at every turn, put every training idea into a real-life example, and by the end of our week had literally changed how all of us felt about our own projects.

It seems in someone's formal statistical adjustment curve, months nine through fourteen are when most Peace Corps volunteers leave service (if they are going to leave). Whether this is the case or not, there was a lot of, "I wonder if I've done the right thing?" going on at the beginning of our St. Lucia training week. Hence, not only was the training timely, it also awakened me again to the fact that all is not as it appears and don't get too shook if things get a little rougher yet!

But all seriousness aside, I loved the trip because we stayed in a guesthouse in an almost quiet neighborhood where our breakfast was served in a big, bright open room with windows all around, curtains blowing in the breeze. After a day of worshipping (a huge, full lunch included). I ended up at a mall complete with fast food choices of Chinese, Mexican and Italian. The mall almost topped having a room to myself and hot water, but not quite. It also turned out to be a real treat to "hang around" with people my own age! There were four of us over fifty from three different islands who swam, watched the sunset and ate together. Marvelous for the soul!

A few of my other adventures this past month included a day trip on the cargo ship Amazing Grace from Portsmouth past Guadalupe and the Saints to Marie Galante then back past the north end of Dominica home to Portsmouth. The boat trip, sponsored by the local Methodist Church as an annual fund raiser, usually draws anywhere from 800 to 1,000 people. Not this year, thank heavens! The boat never docked, just chugged along through the "deep blue sea." I sat most of the trip on a rolled up bale of rope, took a whole roll of slides, ate barbequed chicken and rice, and people watched! We reached Dominica's north end about 4:00 p.m. where the low lying sun etched the jagged cliffs and wind shorn vegetation against an outline of sky dark clouds.

To continue my religious education, I'm taking part in a pilgrimage to Toucare every Tuesday night for nine weeks. I've already missed three Tuesdays out of six: on some the group walks to Toucare, a village four miles north of Portsmouth. Sorry to admit, but I only go when they take a transport which they only take if it looks like rain! This Novena to St. Anthony is held in a brightly painted, turquoise blue, old-fashioned church. Wooden shutters are flung wide open and the sounds of lapping water, night crickets, occasional wind and rain, flood, the church competing with beautiful voices and the visiting Father's sermon.

My favorite evening sermon so far was about two weeks ago when I heard about marriage and divorce and all the laws which govern those things on Dominica. The next day Thomas told us it was customary, at one time, on a man's wedding night, to spread a white sheet on the couple's bed to prove the bride was a virgin. The parents acted as recorders of this event. If the bride was not a virgin, the marriage was called off!

The Toucare pilgrimage is to culminate in the Feast of St. Anthony on June 13th. This used to be the biggest feast and celebration in all of Dominica. I'm not sure how it will all come together this year, but I'll just bet it'll be enjoyable and educational!

We finally have an official ENCORE office! Right on Portsmouth's main street! At first it was difficult to adjust, but it's much better now. We have FANS! The new office makes us more visible to the public and seems much more respectful. One day, after we'd been at the new location for only four days, I wrote the following in my journal, "Long Day! Dr. Chase and her St. Lucia 'group' (Debbie Bushell, technical officer and Sandra, accountant), Ophelia Marie, Thomas Paul, Mrs. Andre, Mel and I all met from 11:00 a.m. to 2:00 p.m. in our 'new' office. Heat, noise and all! Sandra said we had her undying sympathy. The heat was awful, the noise was awful, the subject matter intense!"

Just a few more of my journal images and stories from this past month before I close.

"Today I watched an old man staggering down the street, playing a harmonica and jabbering to himself. Could he ever make that harmonica sing!"

"Everyone I met on way home today had a mango in their mouth? Eunella (Loic's mom) asked Melanie, 'You haven't seen Loic much. Right?' Melanie replied, "No. Did he get in trouble for coming over so much?' Eunella, 'He's a changed boy, you know. Spends all his time in a mango tree. Won't even come down to eat supper, too full of mangos!'"

They are really yummy! And it is the season!

"Waited from 9:15 a.m. until after 1:00 today for a 9:00 a.m. meeting to happen. When it finally did start, I took one page of notes, everyone ordered lunch, then ate! Meeting lasted just about an hour!"

"Each morning this week I simply want to go someplace and curl up. I think of sleeping bags in the mountains by a stream, the sounds, pine trees and softness."

"Sitting on veranda watching little French youngster form Guadalupe 'do his laundry.' He's standing beside a bucket full of water, naked except for underwear, wringing out a pair of his own shorts. Learning how to do your own laundry begins early on Dominica. Marsault is only three!"

"On my way to the bank today, saw a big black dog, dead, in the open drain."

Mary Peterson had company from U.S. for two weeks, one lady was a Peace Corp volunteer on St. Kitts in the 1970s. So Mary invited me over for a weekend. Five women, rain for a whole day and night, and two long (5:45 a.m. to 7:30 a.m. then 8:30 a.m. to 9:30 a.m.) transport rides home via Roseau didn't translate to an outstanding weekend. However, it did have some high points, but when I got home this time I realized how lucky I was: running water, closeness to my work, Melanie as a housemate, kitchen sink, refrigerator, indoor shower and toilet, my own space! So much for my desire to live like Mary on a perpetual camping trip!

At work, we've "sent up" eight project proposals with two more ready for submission! Response from ENCORE higher-ups is not to encouraging, but we're all optimistic. In the meantime, we've started to look at beach clean-ups. I keep asking Thomas, "What in the world would we do if even half of the projects got approved?"

End of Journal Entries

Lori, Caroline, Josh and Kyle are COMING TO VISIT! Think I can get excited?

Many of you write to tell me how much you enjoy my letters and the sharing of this adventure. But I must say, you're a great bunch of adventurers and letter writers yourselves. I enjoy hearing from you so much. Thank you, nice people! Love you, Mary Ann

May 21, 1993

Mom and Bill:

I'm almost embarrassed to mail this letter to you. Before I wrote it, it seemed like ages since my last general letter. But now that it's written, it seems like just yesterday that I sent the April one off.

But I figure it will be Monday before this one goes in the mail. That's the 24th. Then ten days to reach you. That's June 3. Then who knows when you can deal with it. So maybe the time is okay!

I had fun writing – as usual – because Thomas Paul is gone, Melanie and I caught up on all our office work so decided to use computer to type letters. So all you'll have to do is copy and mail. Listen to me, that's all! Thank you again for all you do.

It's been fun hearing from Karlon Lemos since Lloyd and Kathryn are off to New Zealand, et cetera. I got a beautiful lake card from Lloyd in mail yesterday. If New Zealand is half that pretty, it's a dream.

I heard from Auntie Carol who tells me what a good birthday she had: lunches, dinners and all. Nice. Also about her trip on bus to South Shore and visit with Billie and Marshall. How many people do you think do that – visit relatives rather than gamble? If you and Carol do, must be more!

I heard from an old friend today, and in April he went to Jamaica on an elder hostel, but to teach teachers how to identify special Ed students. He worked in a poverty area for two weeks. I've not heard the outcome. He only wrote on his way there.

Also, Sacramento Sierra Club friends went to elder hostel in Arizona and camped on the way there and back – quite an experience: wind, full campgrounds. Evidently the desert is blooming and campers are out in droves!

I need your help, Mom, to resolve an internal problem that I seem to be having. Nothing serious, I'd just like to get to the bottom of it all in my mind – if that is possible. I also need you to tell me exactly how you remember everything – not as you think I might want to hear it. Okay? Anyway, when I was growing up I remember that I never seemed to be right. I was always doing things wrong (not bad things), that in school the boys told me I wasn't smart, but got my grades because I was teacher's pet. I even remember you doing my reports and things like that. Is any of this just my imagination or did I receive lots of put-downs in my early (formative) years? I really appreciate your help! Thanks.

Well, hope the patient is 100% up and about. I keep hearing how beautiful Auburn's spring is to walk in. Enjoy yourselves.

Love, Mary Ann

I'm excited about all coming to Dominica! Have fun at the wedding, too!

June 25, 1993

Dear Family and Friends:

It's about 14:00 (2:00 p.m.) on Friday afternoon. At 10:00 this morning Melanie left for Antigua on her way to a three-week vacation back home. Mr. Paul's out combing the neighborhood for grapefruit to make juice for tomorrow's beach clean-up activity. And there's not a single box of perforated, eight and one-half by eleven inch computer paper on Dominica. So, just like the computer printer, my afternoon projects have come to a screeching halt!

Actually, I still have single sheets of paper that can be fed into the printer but it balks at being given only one page at a time for more than three pages in a row. Thus, printing a proposal for Indian River Tour Guides Training will just have to wait until "someone" on Dominica receives a shipment of computer paper. Our two "most reliable" suppliers have been telling us for at least a month that the paper will be here "next" week. Meanwhile, even our surplus of single sheets is slipping!

Melanie was so excited about going home! Plus, she's already excited about coming back because on August 1 she'll move into her very own two-bedroom house. Her plans for going home taught us both a good lesson – don't tell anyone you're going. EVERYONE wants her to bring them back something: a certain pair of shoes, a Scrabble game, 1,000 pipe cleaners, spray paint. One young man even apologized because he couldn't think of anything for Melanie to bring him!

Everyone is so happy for her, but also worried silly that she may not return. At the same time, they are quite sad for me because I'm all alone! Kenroy's little brother, Ronald, promises to visit me each day to keep me from getting too lonely. During working hours for ENCORE, Melanie's the only one who wears a watch, so now I'll have to listen more attentively to the Church bells to know when to go to lunch. I can't quite trust my stomach because I'm usually hungry by 10:00 a.m. Not sure what to do about quitting time!

There's only one more week of school before summer vacation. This past week the Government School took on a whole new atmosphere: Bingo on Monday night, spelling, math, and general knowledge contests on Tuesday night, sports day practice on Wednesday, students' technical exhibition on Thursday, and all-day sport competitions today, Friday.

In the middle of this exciting school's week, ENCORE teamed up with the local Parliamentary Representative, Mr. Roosevelt (Rosie) Douglas and local community members to launch a massive beach clean-up campaign! Cleaning-up day is tomorrow! Each day this week, Tuesday through Friday between 4:00 p.m. and 6:00 p.m., Mr. Paul and one of Rose's "boys" cruised the streets of a local village in the ENCORE vehicle, loud speakers mounted in the back, sensitizing villagers about each evening's 7:00 public meeting.

Around 7:00 p.m., following each afternoon's meeting announcement, at a pre-determined spot in the appropriate local village, Mr. Paul and Rosie's "boy" set up the trusty pick-up and loud speakers. As the speakers blare forth with the ENCORE calypso song "Environmental Protection" composed by a local high school student Glenroy Jno Baptiste who won the Earth Day song competition, persons start to gather. Somewhere between 7:30 and 8:00 (depending on how many people appear), Mr. Paul begins talking about ENCORE, the environment, Saturday's beach clean-up, and any other thing he deems pertinent. Last night he talked about the small fishes in the sea that he used to be able to reach down and pick up with his hands. They are no longer there!

As the crowd grows other persons speak all on the upcoming beach clean-up and what this will mean to Portsmouth! The plan is to clean five main beaches tomorrow. We've been working with the local Environmental Health Officer who is a member of our ENCORE Local Site Management

Team and a local Beach Clean-up committee. I really shouldn't say "we," it's been mostly Thomas Paul's baby this time!

Last night's public meeting was held as planned in the community of Lagoon. Besides Mr. Paul and Rosie's boy," ENCORE National Coordinator Ophelia Marie spoke along with a local resident who owns the beach "resort" called the Purple Turtle, a school teacher who is also president of the local crafts producers association and very involved with the local tourist industry, our friend Luke who stood in for the Freedom Party Parliamentary Representative, and last but not least, the opposition party's favorite and supposedly their candidate for the next Dominican Prime Minister, Rosei Douglas.

Even though all this drama takes place on a small village street with less than 30 onlookers, it's considered important (serious) business. Not something that is treated lightly! It is interesting, too, to wonder how many persons are listening and not showing themselves! In the dark of the night, this is quite easily done in a Dominican village.

The Beach clean-up campaign settled in, in a most unusual way! We (ENCORE staff and local site management team) discussed the feasibility of just such an activity, when to have it, how to do it, et cetera, et cetera et cetera. The next think we know, true to "Thomas Paul form." He's off and running. First he's rounded up Rosie Doulas to enlist his political clout, and once again the planning, organization, lead-time fly out the window in race of what M. Paul perceives should be done Consequently, he alienates many of his LSMT people, rushes through things like a bull in a China closet, ends up by dong 99% of the work himself which means he's exhausted and lot of promises never quite materialize! I've yet to figure out how much of this behavior is actually cultural and how much the actions of a man motivated by his ego and political aspirations!

To keep myself mentally afloat between being a visitor on the island and trying to be a Peace Corps volunteer working on the ENCORE project. I often resort to day dreaming about moving to another village. This past month, I got a little further than day dreaming I actually had persons looking for housing for me in Vielle case. But the bubble finally burst when I realized ALL my spare time would be spent either on the transport of waiting to get down into Portsmouth to go to work! I think I've mentioned Vieille Case to some of you already. It's where the first Mass was held on Dominica in the 1600s. Where there are lawns and shade trees, wide-wide streets and not a piece of trash in site!

Yesterday, I interviewed a young lady who is going to volunteer in the ENCORE office doing secretarial work in exchange for computer training! I've also been working with Mrs. Andre (the lady who lifts you off the ground when you're hugged and cooks goat water at Christmas time) to a few months back, the Dominican Development Corporation sponsored a local training class in banana art. Many shades of banana plant fibers are cut into various sizes and shapes, glued onto card stock to form numerous scenes or figures depicting such things as: a banana man and hoe, a Carib drummer, parrots, Anthyriums, a Dominican farmer carrying bananas on his head. Depending on the creative ability of the artist, the end product can be a beautiful play of dark against light and soft against rough.

Everyone who has seen the finished banana art cards or wall plaques have been quite taken with them. The minister of Agriculture has even taken card samples to England. Mrs. Andre's plan is to take the trained banana art craftsmen (and women) to the next level by applying for ENCORE funds to help them learn production and marketing skills, form a cooperative, and train new people. I wish them tremendous success. But I'm not sure how good my skills are at fettering out all the necessary parts to put together a workable (realistic) project proposal!

Much of what is done here is in the "Dominica Way" that I've described before or by pie-in-the-sky dreaming (my own perception of realism is not in the Dominican imagination or reality). It's entirely possible (and my jury is still out on this one), but after having unrealistically high expectations, the outcome is simply forgotten. The fun was in the dreaming! Thus, further on down the road, if anything at all is accomplished – everyone is satisfied. The biggest problem with that (for me, not for them) is that ENCORE won't accept a proposal with unrealistic goals or written in less than concrete terms, much less give money to a project that is not submitted in written form. Plus, they expect everything that is proposed to be accomplished! Wish us luck with tomorrow's beach clean-up!

June 27, 1993; 7:30 p.m. Sunday

Dear Mom and Bill:

I'm sitting here writing and realizing that next Sunday and by the time you get this letter, Caroline, Lori and the two boys will be here! Such a thing for me I can hardly imagine. And even more earth shattering for them!

The local friends seem quite excited about it all. They will be the first Peace Corps volunteer's family to be in Portsmouth! This is especially true in having grandsons coming. Most PCVs are young and only bring mothers and fathers! But to have young people seems unusual. We'll see what kind of a stir is created. Probably none at all!

I thought about them all so much yesterday. We had a massive beach clean-up campaign going. My job was to photograph the before and the after. At one point I stopped and watched the fishermen pull in their nets. Josh and Kyle would love that – actually, even Caroline and Lori. One fisherman was so old and frail he could barely pull the rope. They stand and pull for two hours to bring the nets in! Beside small skinny silver fish, they also caught quite a few tin cans and other "dirty bay" matter!

The beach clean-up was fairly successful. Besides photos, I got to barbeque chicken for about three hours. Luckily, I was in a shady spot. The day was fairly cool, and the glare off the Caribbean bearable.

Melanie's found her own house to live in so my turn is next. She's also off to Virginia for a three-week vacation!

I absolutely love it here without her. Very hard to explain and even harder to admit, but the truth.

Thank you for sharing your long-ago memories. From my vantage point of 58 years I really believe your theory that listening to children is important! Wish I had done more of that for my own children.

Thank you, Bill, for note on my "unsent" Newsweek letter. Today I want to write President Clinton about the missile attack on Iraq!

I almost have another general letter ready, but promise not to send it too soon!

Take care! I heard the wedding was HOT. The Caribbean will be cool to the family.

Love, Mary Ann

P.S. Mom, I'm looking forward to seeing your photos. Karlon really loved her private art show!

June 28, 1993 Monday

On Saturday, a successful day was had by all including yours truly! Lots of beach got cleaned, lots of shrubs cleared out, lots of trash hauled off, and lots of chicken cooked and eaten! I took photographs from one end of Portsmouth to the other – before clean-up and after clean-up! In between photos, I barbequed chicken for at least three hours! "Good job." I was told! "Tasty chicken!"

Actually, it was fun because at first the ladies I helped at the Purple Turtle Beach Resort were afraid to let me do anything. Finally, they decided I could help cook the chicken. Little did they know what an old hand I am at barbequing chicken. But even I'll admit this was the first time I'd barbequed on a huge grill, set about 15 feet from the Caribbean Sea, while standing on a cement block spearing chicken legs and thighs, my "boobs" heated by hot coals as gobs or smoke curled about my hair and face! The chicken took forever to cook. But the smells spread instantly, and about every ten minutes children, wet from the sea, crowded around to see how much longer they'd have to wait!

Last week there was talk of moving the ENCORE office again. (Another story for the telling when I get home.) Thomas kept saying we were going to move at night so no one would see us move. When I asked why we didn't want anyone to see us, especially since that would be a good way to advertise we had a new location, he replied, "There's a stigma connected with moving in Dominica. The only reason you move is because you haven't paid your rent. So you don't want anyone to see you. And if it's a house you're moving out of, you don't want your neighbors to see your belongings (like an old tattered mattress), because that's knowing your business."

Last Sunday I was invited to be a panel member for the Northern District Progressive Women's Club's celebration of Family Month. The topic was "Broken Families, its causes, effects, prevention and solutions." Quite a mouthful and quite an education for me! About 30 women made up the audience. A local lay minister and I made up the panel. Four persons were originally scheduled, but only the two of us showed up.

Because Dominica is such a religious stronghold, many of the problems such as early pregnancies, broken families, drugs and alcohol are blamed on "moving away from God or not living in God's plan." I'm not one to argue at all with that point. However, it often keeps leaders from looking for other causes, effects, and solutions to very serious problem. But I enjoyed being on the panel, and in this case, listening to the differing opinions between the young women and the older women. If you don't already know, women on Dominica (even though looked up to and loved) are truly at the mercy of a male-dominated society.

Since I last wrote to you, still on the religious theme, I've experienced the phenomenon as "evil spirits." I haven't written home too much about this very strange happening and won't say too much here. (one more home-telling story.) But the spirits began "appearing" in Portsmouth about the time of the Charismatic Conference in Roseau and continued their random wanderings for the next few weeks.

Things have quieted down completely now! But I sure remember all the yelling and screaming and rumors floating about on what it all meant and how an evil spirit can enter your body if you don't live right, especially if you're a priest or a young women who hasn't prayed and fasted enough!

The Portsmouth victims were all young, very religious Catholic women, a number of them still students at the St. John's School. The arrival of the evil spirits coincided with the strenuous "end of the year" exams as well as the Easter season. The final rumor (that I heard) was that the whole thing was "caused" or "directed at" discrediting the current acting principal of St. John's School so the powers that be would bring the nuns back to run the school. Believe it or not, this September the nuns return.

The most bizarre part of the spirit story concerns one of the students at St. John's School whom "the spirit entered." A the story goes, she was taken to the local medical clinic in bad shape – her body rigid, hair standing on end, not at all herself, talking in a strange voice shouting that she was going to kill her father! Holy Cow! Needless to say, this story (repeated to me by the local Environmental Health officer whom I admire, who doesn't believe in evil spirits and who witnessed the whole event almost made a believer out of me!

Many of you continue to ask, "What is your job?" I think I've about decided that my job (not just mine, but the other two ENCORE PCVs, Mark and Melanie, too) is to pave the way for any and all Peace Corps volunteers who get assigned to ENCORE on Dominica over the next five years – (if any get assigned). We three definitely don't have a typical Peace Corps project, but then does anyone! In our case, however, we never did have a stated project as such. We were simply assigned to the ENCORE project which was run sometimes successfully, sometimes not so successfully. I'm sure that won't help answer your question. But it's the best I can do.

We've had a number of meetings with higher-ups – everyone's higher than we are – from our own boss, Thomas Paul, to Ophelia Marie to the Associate Peace Corps Director on Dominica to finally the Eastern Caribbean Peace Corps Country Director from St. Lucia. Everyone got fairly shook up about all of this, especially when we were paid a visit by the head man or USAID in charge of ENCORE. Things are now in a state of flux, and I'm not at all sure how they will settle out. For one thing, there are way too many chickens in the broth or fish in the stew! Even the head ENCORE lady in St. Lucia got in on the act. It is common knowledge that "the Peace Corps are not happy!" I think it's also becoming common knowledge that "the Peace Corps" are troublesome!

In August ENCORE is getting a new PCV to replace Chadwick, the young woman who returned home in January. I've asked if they would consider moving me to Scott's Head in the south and assigning the new volunteer (a young man) to Portsmouth. Most of the hurdles for such a move have been jumped. So before I send this letter off in the mail, I may know if I'll fly south for my second year or stay in Portsmouth. At first, when the idea surfaced, I really wanted to move to Scott's Head. But now, after so many obstacles and uncovered ramifications, I'll certainly understand if I stay in Portsmouth.

This coming weekend is the Fisherman's Feast – the Feast of St. Peter. Supposedly, Portsmouth will be alive with fun, food, and canoe races. The racing teams come from Guadalupe and Martinique to race their handmade Gommler canoes. In the midst of all this fun and frolic, Lori, Caroline, Josh and Kyle arrive at 1:30 on Sunday at Canefield Airport. They'll have some wild stories about Canefield!

June 29, 1993

Dear Melanie;

I'll try to keep my handwriting legible and my spelling correct! This is the first time in three and a half days my hands haven't been stiff! I barbequed chicken at the Purple Turtle for three plus hours on Saturday!

It seems Mrs. Alexis was going to cook all the Lagoon food (according to T.P.), but changed her mind. So Vincent said Priscilla would do it. She went all over to find charcoal because she was out. I think she ended up getting it in Borne. Then she started chicken late and when I offered to help, I got to cook. I really enjoyed it! And it was delicious!

The young people who came with Thomas to help clean ended up bathing before lunch and after lunch. He probably got maybe three hours of work out of them which wasn't bad considering there were very few tools and no juice until 12:30 or so!

Everyone seems to feel the day was satisfactory. Although some say it could have been better. And of course T.P. says, "You don't listen to those!"

Everyone asks of you. And the real reason for the letter is to tell you it looks like I'm going to Scott's Head. We had an "emergency" staff meeting today in Roseau to discuss the situation. My relationship with Thomas as deteriorated daily! But I had still settled myself down to staying in Portsmouth.

It seems Felix G. told Ophelia that the decision was hers to make and she was to simply tell Dr. Chase that this was the decision she had reached.

At the meeting, Ophelia probed and prodded until a lot surfaced. Mark even apologized to Val for talking in front of Dr. Chase and Gus. I was so proud of him! His voice shook and all, but he kept right on and said his say very nicely.

The typing issue came up and Ophelia said she felt that was masking the real problem. I spoke and said I felt that the team spirit that we'd begun with had deteriorated and I was trying to discover the reason for this.

Ophelia asked T.P. how he felt about that, if it were true. He said he guessed so ever since the PCVs got together and complained to the higher-ups! Ophelia said he could turn in his reports handwritten and Ginnette would type them – that the Peace Corps were not secretaries!

On the way home, T.P. was (quite vexed)

P.S.S. Murphy says you just transfer telephone and ask for a name charge – cost is $150.00. He wrote transfer on your app. All you do is write a letter when you return.

July 15, 1993

Lori, Caroline, Josh and Kyle arrived, but not at 1:30 on Sunday! After a mix-up at the Sacramento Airport on Saturday and many hours of standby on Antigua, a tired but happy Lori, Caroline and Kyle arrived at Dominica's Canefield Airport at 2:30 on Monday the 5th. Josh had flown in all by himself early in the morning with a note from Lori but no luggage! Both his luggage and Caroline's were missing. Even after it finally got to Dominica we couldn't pick it up until late Wednesday because on Tuesday we went hiking in the Cabrits National Forest, swimming at Secret Beach and "canoeing" up the Indian River. That night we got the rental car, but Lori couldn't drive it until she got a permit (her International Driver's License meant nothing)! But easier said than done. The permit books were off to Roseau for auditing. Welcome to Dominica!

You'll have to talk to the four of them to get their perspective on the trip. But I loved every minute they were here as hard as it was at times – like when they left! Plus, I'm used to moving at a snail's pace. But did things ever pick up when we rented the car. Seeing everyone was ever so special. In fact, seeing the excitement in Josh's eyes when he first stepped off the plane made my past year seem worth it all!

We went to places on the island that I'd never seen. Yet in looking back, we probably didn't spend enough time just hanging around, although many games of Crazy Eights got played! Lori took to driving on the left-hand side of the road quite easily, but that still left the glare, hills, narrow roads, lack of guardrails, rain, potholes, curves, other drivers and tremendous concentration; not to mention headlights and dodging land crabs. They were all such troopers from cold showers to doing ALL the laundry by hand! We had a pretty good storm one day but didn't even know it at the time we'd spent most of the day at the beach!

I guess one of the nicest things I heard about their visit was from Kenroy. He said, "I'm finding them quite nice people. Seems maybe they're getting that from you." Kenroy and I along with many, many others, wish they could have stayed longer! Ask Lori about how the little Dominican and French girls took after Kyle. One even chased him around a power pole! And ask Josh about his new pen pal. Just so you don't think the young boys had all the fun – a very handsome local organic farmer invited Caroline to come live with him! And with Lori at the wheel, we never had a bit of trouble pulling into the oncoming traffic – somehow the vehicles always stopped to let her in!

I can't believe I started this letter 20 days ago! Melanie's due back next Wednesday. On Friday I'm off to Grenada with Mary Peterson for a week's vacation. We'll stay with Peace Corps volunteers on Grenada. We finally have a new box of computer paper, but now the printer ribbon needs re-inking! The man who we rent our equipment from is off island for a week or two, so I still haven't printed the Indian River Tour Guide Training proposal. I'm going to see if I can get it re-inked while I'm in Roseau tomorrow for a Peace Corps meeting.

It does look like I'll spend my second year in Scott's Head. Right now the local site manager in Scott's Head is trying to locate a house for me to move into about the first of August. When I think about the change, I vacillate between happy and sad: happy because it seems the right thing to do and sad because I'm leaving all my friends in Portsmouth. A number of them seem quite upset that the Portsmouth ENCORE site is losing what they call "benefit of my maturity and expertise."

The Fishermen's Feast in Portsmouth was right out of the storybooks – not done for the tourist but for the fishermen of Portsmouth! A special mass dedicated to St. Peter was held at 9:00 a.m. on Sunday where all of the food for a feast (including a platter of fish, fruits, cakes and ground provisions) was carried up the aisle by the fishermen and their wives all dressed in costumes. Following the offering, a Fisherman of the Year was honored and a small slice of cake served to everyone in the church. After mass, the priest and congregation moved (walked) to the bayside where five blue fishing boats were "decked out" in yellow and red flowers held together by masses of greenery.

After blessing the fishing boats lined up on the beach, the Father sprinkled holy water all around as a single blue boat, guided by a tall dark fisherman dressed in a white suit, sliced delicately through the blue Caribbean waters. When it came to rest the bayside, in climbed the priest, a young girl, a small child (carried by a young fisherman), and another fisherman holding a wreath of flowers. All this time, a jing bing band played a snappy tune as the fishermen and their wives, dressed in colors that matched the sea and flowers, mingled between the blue boats.

As the fisherman held the wreath high above his head, the boatman guided the small cart out to the middle of the bay where the flowers were tossed overboard and the water blessed. I kept telling myself, "I'm not a bystander, I'm a part of this!" Oh, yes, the racing canoes never showed up!

Love and peace to each of you.
New address:
PCV Mary Ann Kollenberg
P.O. Box 357
Roseau, Commonwealth of Dominica, West Indies

July 30 – Giraudel.

I'm at PCV Charles' house in Giraudel, a halfway move to Scott's Head. My house won't be ready until August 5. Thomas Paul said Felix Gregoire (Permanent Secretary of Agriculture) gave his blessings today to my new placement, and today was the day to move! So we moved! In the rain! The sky is a soft peach with grey clouds laying softly over the pale blue of a twilight sky. I feel like I'm still on vacation and there is a three-day holiday still to look forward to. It's so special to be here: quiet, birds before sunset, cool.

It rained all day, almost. We (Thomas Paul, Melanie and I) packed the ENCORE vehicle in Portsmouth between downpours then unpacked in Giraudel between cloudbursts. I must get up early tomorrow and go to market in Roseau or I won't have any food for the weekend.

(Charles is on vacation, island hopping. Nice of him to offer house.) Such mixed feelings leaving

Portsmouth. I bid the house goodbye. It looked nice inside, fresh and clean. I didn't feel like I was leaving because we go to down the road so often. On Dominica it's hard to tell friends goodbye, that's you're leaving. They don't like to hear that. Besides, July 1992's memories are still too close for comfort.

August 6; Scott's Head

Such days these have been! Today up at 5:30. Thought I'd overslept. It's lighter here at 5:30 than in Giraudel. Last night was such a strange one. Went upstairs at 8:00 p.m. and some rearranging, then to bed to read. Mattress not the best, but figured I'd get used to it. It was a hot night, my first night in Scott's Head, mosquitoes all around. Even the mattress seemed to give off heat! I tried plugging in the fan without an adapter. It didn't work. Finally came downstairs, found adapter, but fan still wouldn't work in my room. So I moved into another bedroom, put fan on and finally slept. Tonight is different. Downstairs is friendlier. Mark came by and left his bicycle on front porch while he got to a meeting. He'll ride home in the dark with my flashlight.

From my new "digs" its ten minutes to the bus stop on Scott's Head Main Street, all downhill! This morning I was in a transport by 7:30, in Roseau by 8:00. Went first to bank, then dropped firm at photo lab, then to 9:00 doctor's appointment. Out at 11:00. Next went to Peace Corps office where I met Mark who typed 1993-94 annual ENCORE work plan for Scott's Head/Soufriere/Gallion (my new local site). I took copies to Ministry for secretary, then to get a mug shot for my second-year work permit. Picked up prints at lab and went to Jolly's Pharmacy for prescriptions. To lunch at Orchard House (my favorite spot) then to open market, grocery store, and bakery and back to bus stop to catch Scott's Head transport. Dr. Allport said my circulation was excellent! "Are you walking a lot?' she asked. Ha! Ha!

When I got on the transport it took quite a while to fill up and I worried my frozen chicken and turkey drumsticks would thaw. Turkey did. We stopped twice on way home for bread and once for gasoline. Passengers give driver money for bread and verbal orders – "six 75 cent loaves, three one dollar loaves." Driver comes back with correct number of loaves, passes them through the window with the correct change to the right person! At the gas station everyone bought sliced watermelon. Quite a sight. Fifteen grown-ups dripping watermelon juice down their chins and spitting seeds. And, of course, as we finished, out the window went the rind.

Finally leaving the gas station, the driver drove like a bat out of his cave, careening around curve after curve. As we came around one curve, a huge boulder sat smack in the middle of the road. It didn't look like there was enough space for him to pass on our side.

Sure enough, he swung the bus to the right (ocean side) just in time to see a small blue car coming towards us heading directly in our path. Without blinking an eye, our driver veered back to the left, never slowed down, and whizzed between the boulder and the cliff. I counted my blessings all the way to Scott's Head. In fact, I'm still counting them! Someone recently commented that transport rides are the reason faith is so strong on Dominica.

August 8; Scott's Head

I'm writing by candlelight. Power's off. Plumber's here fixing leak under bathtub. Yesterday he fixed upstairs toilet. Hurrah! I don't have to come downstairs in the middle of the night anymore! Rainbow this morning from Caribbean to Atlantic. I love looking out and seeing the small fishing boats in their accustomed spots on the "bank" early in the morning, watching the bay on my way to work in Soufriere and realizing what a unique experience this all really is! Also, I've decided for now that I'm doing Mr. Eli a favor by living in his house. This attitude helps keep the guilt away.

August 10; Scott's Head

Yesterday a big storm! Rain and wind all day. First it was called a depression, then at 5:00 p.m. it was upgraded to a tropical storm 30 miles east of Martinique. I closed the house up tight like I was advised on the radio, put slacks and a T-shirt on, even brought socks downstairs to put on if it got cold. I got concerned when I looked outside because none of the houses around me had on lights! Had everyone left! No mention on radio of storm upgrading to a hurricane. (Storm has winds of 30-73 miles per hour. Hurricane, 74 miles per hour or more.) In fact, after 5:00 p.m. no mention was made of storm at all! Winds died down about 9:00 a.m. and in the morning all was calm, at least at Scott's Head. When I went to church the northwest sky appeared dark and ominous. Caribbean turned a deep dark blue, sky almost blue-black. I could see rain pouring from the darkness moving in sheets across the sea.

This afternoon, the "girls" (seven young girls' ages four to thirteen who have befriended me) took me on a picnic at Tou Sab (a favorite snorkeling spot in Scott's Head). Left house about 2:30—nice outside, clouds lingering further north but looked good over Scott's Head. About an hour later, after we'd gone swimming (bathed), devoured watermelon and oatmeal cookies. It began to rain, pour, water came out of the sky and plopped all around us: on clothes, food, camera, us and the sea. Goosebumps appeared on everyone. We stood under trees until the trees were drenched. We tried to get organized but everything was so wet. The girls jumped back into the sea to get warm while I put on my clothes, last of all wet leather tennis shoes. Then off across the spit we walked, through the village. Men playing dominoes outside a shop under shelter gave us a big hand. By this time my blue denim skirt stuck to my knees and thighs, my shoes and the wet T-shirt matched my plastered hair! As we went up the series of concrete paths that make up the village, water cascaded down drainpipes off rooftops and ran in torrents down the walkways. As we trudged ever upward, the girls stopped under every downspout for a fresh shower. We walked straight up each miniature rushing stream – the water coming so fast and thick I'm surprised we didn't run into any white water. Two young men coming downhill in yellow slickers told us we looked beautiful! This maze of winding, steep concrete walkways not only give access to the village, but also drains it!

Just last night I'd stood at my upstairs window looking out on the storm down at the spit watching the Atlantic wind-whipped shore wishing I could be there, walking, feeling the wind, the sound and power. But "No," I said, "the villagers will think you're crazy." Today, I proved it!

August 16; Scott's Head

I like Scott's Head. I like the way its main street looks, its color, the sea, the small colorful fishing boats, the men playing dominoes in the shade under trees or shop awnings. There are more birds in my yard, big lizards, and land crabs. And slowly I will get to know the people.

August 27; Scott's Head

Proven once again that what will happen in a day is never known ahead of time, nor is the day over until it's over! Up this morning at 5:30, showered, dressed, ate breakfast and out the door to Mark's house. Caught transport at 7:20. Arrived early at Mark's where food would be prepared for second day of sulfur deposit trail clearing project. (Formal name is Trail Rehabilitation and Stabilization.) Mark had just finished washing pots and pans left from yesterday. All plastic cups and plates still left to wash: So I did!

The "girls" (Volunteers of ENCORE working group) came just as I finished last dish and preparation began on food for today. The clearing crew came by at 9:00 and took snacks (juice and sandwiches) with them. The crew would walk almost two miles before they began clearing the trail.

We worked all morning on lunch, cooking, chopping, and washing. They let me make paleau (rice and chicken), all the while giving me precise directions. I now know two more local dishes because I helped with the second dish, meal in one pot; chicken dumplings, potatoes, red beans, macaroni and seasonings! Yummy stuff. About 12:30 we ate and waited for Val to come and haul us and the food to project site. When we finally arrived, the poor folks were about famished.

A group of us then set out to evaluate the project's progress. After driving another mile, we walked up the cleared trail past two lower sulfur deposits to the highest one. We walked by snake caves (no snakes, they sleep all day, I'm told), large lizards (I haven't seen I Iguana yet – keep hoping), two hawks, hot steam sulfur crystal mounds, all inside an ancient eroded volcanic crater. Our destination, the highest sulfur deposit also contains a waterfall. From this point we looked back from where we'd come, out towards a long valley reaching to the Atlantic. Clear day, Martinique in the distance.

Every day there seems to be more to see and explore. After hike Mark and I returned to kitchen and, once again, cleaned all the pots, pans, plastic cups and red plastic plates! I'm due to go to my first Scott's Heads Youth Group meeting tonight at 7:00 p.m. Not sure my legs will carry me.

September 1; Scott's Head

I didn't sleep well last night. Hope tonight will be better. Last night, just before I went upstairs to read, I caught a glimpse of slender brown hairy things poking out from the cupboard door under the kitchen sink. They looked exactly like spider legs I'd seen in the extra bedroom last weekend.

Cautiously opening the door, I confirmed my suspicions! For lack of a better name, I call them wolf spiders. They are dark brown, hairy and from leg tip to leg tip about three inches across. Pondering the situation, I remembered how fast the bedroom spider had climbed the broom handle, which got dropped post haste! Thus, I'm so sad to say, I resorted to Bug Bomb on the "under-the-sink" spider. No sooner had I closed the door on Mr. Spider's gas chamber than a lizard dropped from his perch on my kitchen window landing on the windowsill right by my hand posed to turn on the faucet.

And if that wasn't enough "heart starters" for one night, I heard a deep "hello" at the front of the house. Asking "who's there?" I found out it was friend and neighbor Keagan Adams whom I asked to come around to the back door. Upon opening the back door, what should I see but a lost land crab trying to get away from the porch light I'd just switched on. Unsuccessful in finding his hole, he'd scrunched himself into a corner trying to disappear.

When I first moved into the house it was full of ants – tiny little things crawling purposefully along the walls, in the cracks, under rugs, along the countertops. After a week or more I decided this must stop. So I invested in Bug Bomb. I sprayed a few squirts here and there half-heartedly to see if the chemical had any effect. Bu two nights later, attracted by my inside lights, bugs I'd never seen and some I've become familiar with flew in, danced around in sight – carried off by many, many tiny ants. Since then the little guys and I coexist quite nicely. Must find a way to do the same with Mr. Spider!

I just heard a noise outside and upon investigating saw a man crashing around in the back yard. He said, "Goodnight. I thought there was a snake, but it's only a stick." I asked him if he knew anything about the big spiders. He said I should spray my bedroom every night before to bed. And, he added, I was in real trouble if a centipede bit me during the full moon!

Over the past year I've changed. I'm now happy over the smallest gain, and, most days, content with just being. The new Peace Corps volunteers arrived and were sworn in on August 31. There are 13 new ones. So now we are 23 in all. During the swearing-in ceremony we all sang "The Star Spangled Banner." I've never experienced in my whole life the feeling I had at that moment about my country, my home, myself. The feelings overwhelmed me – the love, the missing, the knowing that a year (ten months actually) must go by before I'd see all of that. But it's even more than "that." It's the mountains, desert, cool winds, cold rain, ocean, people, family, friends, soil and oak trees, dry grass of summer, autumn's colors and spring green buckeye and bluebells.

Peace and Love, Mary Ann
Address:
P.O. Box 357
Roseau
Commonwealth of Dominica
West Indies
Phone number: 1-809-448-0789

September 11, 1993

Dear Family and Friends:

Would you believe I now live on an ancient volcano! A few weeks ago when Peace Corps flew me to St. Lucia, the plane headed southeast from the Canefield Airport along the Dominican coastline direct past Scott's Head, my new home. That day the early morning light and clarity of the air etched all the volcanic ridges, craters and peaks in a spectacular relief. I saw the village of Scott's Head, Soufriere Bay, the land mass known as Scott's Head Point, the spit separating the Atlantic Ocean from the Caribbean Sea. I even spotted my house on the slope.

The peaks surrounding a crater, one mile north of Scott's (better known as the Soufiere Valley where I work), are the highest peaks around the area. But at Scott's Head the Volcanic Cone seemed to rise right up out of the sea.

I am satisfied with my move. Both villages, Soufriere (where I work) and Scott's Head (where I live), offer me a completely different experience than Portsmouth did. Much simpler, basic people live here in these two fishing villages where lots of Creole is spoken and tourism has yet to taint the villagers' outlook. I feel, at times, like I'm in a totally different country!

The ENCORE local site manager, Val Nicholas, also lives in Scott's Head. My Peace Corps volunteer counterpart, Mark Jordan, calls Soufriere home. Val has lived most of his live in Scott's Head. Mark is from southern California but went to college with Melanie at University of Virginia. Coincidence!

And as for Melanie. She is having a rough time right now. But she's a strong young lady. I think all will work out. The doctor has just prescribed ten days of sick leave for her in hopes that it will cure a most uncomfortable rash he feels is stress related.

Because so much time has gone since my last letter, I've decided to copy excerpts from my journal pages written over the last two months. This way you may get a clearer understanding of what I've come to call "my transition." I feel finally, after a year, almost myself; and if I can give that feeling a source it would be in the following order: acceptance, family visit, and move to Scott's Head, vacation and home to look forward to in less than a year.

ENCORE'S NOT CHANGED! But at this local site we've started a project called "Trail Rehabilitation and Stabilization." Soon Mark and I will begin a new "Schools Environmental Education" program and more beach clean-ups. I travel to Roseau at least two times a week for computer work at the main ENCORE office. One of each day's delights is the transport ride! How's that for a switch!

My house is a mansion! All furnished and equipped in uptown style. Water is captured by cistern, but I carry it in a bucket for washing. Some people have been known to pay huge sums of money for my view; and if all of you visited at one time I could probably put you up! Why my luck? It was the only house available in Scott's Head and it belongs to Val's uncle, Mr. Eli, who gave me a deal that was hard to pass up.

Journal Entry I'll begin way back I Portsmouth on July 29th

Arrived home from a week's vacation on Grenada around 12:30 today. Mary Peterson and I stayed last night at Roy Don's guest house in Grand Anse, Grenada – fun, good decision! We had come over from Grenville Wednesday morning and got to St. Georges (Grenada's capitol) around noon. Took our bags to Roy Don's and returned to St. Georges where I bought a local painting, a watercolor of a donkey on a path, and ate lunch in an Italian restaurant overlooking the harbor, just like the Mediterranean!

Vacation good. I relaxed, seemed no one pulling on me. Feels like I've been gone six months. Lots of mail waiting full of sad, sad news of too many friends. I want to call them all and offer words of encouragement.

I have a different perspective on Dominic now. Jermaine (PCV we stayed on Grenville, Grenada) is in a different world than Mary and I. She lives in a fancy house, is slowly going crazy with her job (training a secretariat for the St. Andrew's Foundation) and her current responsibilities on the Rainbow Festival Committee; plus she's having an intimate relationship with the committee's president!

Grenada is quite poor in spots, not as "clean" as Dominica, although it's doing some great things with its national parks. Sand flies and mosquitoes bad! Mary and I cooked a lot, beachcombed, browsed around St. Georges, learned the transportation system and saw most of the island.

End of Journal Entry

October 16, 1993

Dear Mom and Bill:

I certainly enjoyed talking with you on the phone. And again, thank you for typing and sending out letters and ALL! I re-read the latest today and it sounded good. So either I'm not quite as critical today or I've put some distance between the words and author. Fun!

You should be in New York, I believe, as I write this, or at least in Chicago. Aunt Billie and Uncle Marshall called this past week in the evening and said they'd talked to you, too.

I'm happy you can read my printed words and that that makes for "easier" typing. We've been "promised" a laptop computer and printer for the office. That will be fun again if it materializes. Everything is so couched in doubts these days, I put promised in brackets.

Whatever you did to comment (story) about bus, boulder, right and left-hand side of the road worked fine. I've even received comments on scariness of the trip from two of my correspondents. They've also enjoyed spider and bug stories.

I keep hearing pig squeals out my kitchen and dining room windows today. They seem to be coming from across upper road past the vacant lot next to my house. One day I had a bull tethered in a vacant lot. So pigs wouldn't surprise me at all. A man named Mr. Corbett ties his goats along the road each day. I'm watching them head home (down the hill) each evening when he unties them. Two younger ones are never tethered, only the mother. She runs down the hill following her offspring, her canvas-like rope dragging behind.

I've gotten over flu completely and feel quite good, physically and mentally. Sure hope this last for a while. I attended a community group meeting last evening with SHIC (Scott's Head

Improvement Committee). They (as the President described what was happening) really gave me blows about ENCORE! Lucky for me, my emotional state was strong because they certainly verbally let their criticisms fly. What a lesson in detaching!

One of my Sierra College friends wrote and commented on the mild warm fall so far. I'm curious to see how long that last for you. Has color hit New York yet? A delight for my eyes here is watching storms move through the Martinique Channel. They move quite fast and can get very, very dark!

Hope all was as you had expected.

Love, Mary Ann

October 24, 1993

Dear Pat:

Both your October 10 and September 2 letters arrived this past week. Can you figure that out? That means I now know all about the "John swimming mouse: and your lovely sharing of yourself and feelings. Thank you. I feel honored.

You know, all this time I believed you were doing the publicity for the Black and White Ball! Was "Dance Under the Stars" in Newcastle? I wish I had an excuse for my mess-up. But I have not one! I'm glad both were successful. Yes, you told me you were to do a photo booth. Now that can be advertising for "Patricia's Pictures!" What a great idea. But you always say, "I don't know how you have time to do all you do Mary Ann!" Now it's my turn – you sound like a busy, busy lady. But it all sounds like pressure. I hope it isn't the trips and sightseeing and visiting.

From my perch here on this small island where a trip to Roseau is a big deal. Mammoth, the Rush's cabin, wine country and a baroque concert sound like more pure pleasure than this PCV could handle. You know how I go to pieces over hot water. But I loved reading every word. Not only that, I understand exactly what you said about having "the sudden realization that I wanted to belong to someone! I wanted to be special to someone!"

I have felt that way often in my 15 years of singlehood. And those feelings always overwhelm me when I've experienced the closeness of someone special. But I've never taken the time to discover the reality or aftermath, as I call it, of those feelings.

One of my most difficult times on Dominica happened over those feelings. When I lived in Portsmouth I got so lonely for male companionship and conversation – it was a need that simply could not be filled. It (they) finally disappeared as I came to terms with the futility of it all! Do you think when I get back home, I'll have this insatiable appetite for MEN?! Just like I do now for hot water?

But back to the serious business. Your behavior, as you called it, was certainly becoming to a woman of your "age." (Whatever age means anymore.) And from what I understand, we never change! That is when we are attracted to someone! Plus, dear heart, you're so attractive, too!

I've just re-read your letter. It reads like a romantic story. Fun! But serious business and, you're right, "What life is all about." I remember dating a man, recently bereaved, just as I've gone with men recently divorce. And again, you are so right – they have work to do! If their work is not done then you become too involved. (I don't mean just a trip together or whatever), you work hard, too! In some cases it may be worth it – in all of mine it was not. I did the work – or was there while they did the work they needed to do – and when it was done they were gone with another woman who did not know them as I did! They could start fresh. It took me so long to learn these lessons. I'm a slow learner! Let's just hope if there is a next time (and I hope there is), I'll remember all that I've learned.

I don't mean a next time for being the one to help with the work, but a next time to be attractive to a man. I'm torn constantly about the desire to marry and/or to stay single. My single life has been one of such growth and accomplishment on my part, I'd hate to give that up. Yet, ideally a person always thinks they won't have to. That we can be fortunate and meet a lover and a friend. As I tell myself, "Dream on Mary Ann."

November 14, 1993

Dear Family and Friends:

One of my favorite writers, Rainer Maria Rilke, wrote: "... try to love the <u>questions themselves</u> as if they were locked rooms or books written in a foreign language. Don't search for the answers, which could not be given you now, because you would not be able to live them. And the point is, to live everything. <u>Live</u> the questions now. Perhaps then, someday far in the future, you will gradually, without even noticing it, live your way into the answer."

These words written on July 16, 1903, by a German poet, touch me 90 years later on a small tropical island in the Eastern Caribbean. <u>Live the questions</u> I do! However, I've yet to learn 100% to stop asking them first. But time and ENCORE are improving my skill!

The days, weeks, months keep on moving by. The holidays have come again, and this letter brings with it my greetings for a joyous season, one filled with contentment and love for all of you.

As in your lives, much has happened in this part of the world since I last wrote. Our L.S.M.T. (Local Site Management Team) has elected a full executive board including a secretary! (They've only had a chairperson up until now.) Melanie's doing quite well, her rash and stress completely gone. The girls "from up the hill" and I've had a "falling out." But it had to happen sooner or later – they are ever so aggressive and domineering!

I'm working with a group of young men (basketball players) to put on a "Transport" competition for the young boys at Scott's Head. Youngsters nine to fifteen build small wooden hand maneuvered carts they call transports out of scrounged parts and lumber. Peace Corps has a fund that I can use to purchase prizes (in this case, school books). About five years ago, the young basketball players all built transports of their own so they are quite excited about judging a new crop.

The Dominica Environmental Health Department's been holding meetings in Scott's Head on developing a model "double vaulted" pit latrine project for villagers and a plan to eliminate dumping trash into the sea. The health officer works with the Scott's Head Improvement Committee (SHIC) and wants ENCORE to help repair trash bins, known locally as Skips. Eight families are building latrines so far!

Sunsets have been spectacular, made up sometimes of endless pink cotton candy clouds. Plus, the low fall light continues to intensify shadows and the variations in green, making the island appear so dramatic!

On October 27 we learned that ENCORE had just one more year to prove itself under its current St. Lucia management, so word was move ahead at high speed! This past Friday, just 16 days later, we're told, "no one can spend an ENCORE dime! We're out of money until certain financial reports get submitted!

In between we've held two more beach clean-ups; continued work on the Trail Rehabilitation Project and Environmental Education programs; begun a new beach enhancement project at Soufriere Bay involving a hot water springs catchment, clearing, and landscaping; and put on a proposal writing workshop, day to day, however, my greatest satisfaction comes in working with this SHIC, school children, environmental health officer, and the basketball team.

Two "older" Peace Corps volunteers, Polly Zimpel and Nora Stetson, chose to call it quits! Polly left in September to take care of her sick mother. Nora, who is 64, left in late October because she felt very unhappy, homesick and questioned her usefulness as a PCV on Dominica. I had become friends with Nora in the short time that she'd been on the island. She came with the new group in August. We talked a lot, after she'd made her decision, and I've come to believe it was not an easy task deciding to return home after investing so much time and energy in getting into the Peace Corps. Nora, a newly retired nurse, moved to the U.S. from Ireland at 19. She told me her homesickness at 19 was nothing like she'd been experiencing on Dominica. I could relate!

Last Sunday, and only a week after the LSMT elected an executive board, the chairperson, Mr. Hobson Francis, died. He was 70 years old. The funeral, my first on Dominica, was yesterday. At least 500 people attended the service in the Soufriere Catholic Church where more people stood outside than fit inside. I arrived early enough to get a seat, by a fan! And except for my off-white leather tennis shoes I dressed appropriately in white skirt and dark blouse.

Such an affair! Such a tribute to a humble, hard-working caring man. The service began with a tape of Michael Jackson's "Will You be There" followed by two hours of hymns mass, tributes, and the eulogy. Then the wreath-draped casket was wheeled outside, loaded into the back of a bright yellow Toyota pickup, and transported to the cemetery on a knoll just behind the church with all 500 of us following on foot. The ridges of the Soufriere Crater, which form this small valley, towered as sentinels over Mr. Francis' grave that overlooked the sea and the village, with greenery on the hillside above and beyond. The family invited everyone to their home following the funeral!

Since last I've written, I've also done things like sit on a stone wall after work, waiting for a transport to Scott's Head, counting the electrical wires branching out from one main power pole in the village of Soufriere. There are 53!

One Saturday I had lunch with a Walt and Barbara Tindell who have a summer house at Lake Alta (yes in northern California). Walt's in Dominica on a USAID project to help diversify the Eastern Caribbean's Produce Market, anything goes but the banana! Barbara served us an exquisite lasagna, salad, homemade bread lunch while Walt and I talked Placer County Fruit Industry history in front of a color T.V. in their plush home on Morne Daniel just outside of Roseau. The Tindells also lived in Placerville, Sacramento, and even Loomis before moving to Fresno in the early '80s where he worked for Blue Ancho Fruit Exchange Association.

One of the most beautiful spots on this island is located in the mountains above Roseau, a place called Springfield Plantation, where tropical plant and rain forest research gets carried out by persons from around the world. In the middle of October all of us ENCORE Peace Corps wrangled an invitation to an island-wide environmental workshop for Primary Science teachers. It was held at Springfield. Not only did the day's activities happen on an old historic plantation (now conference center and guest house) in the middle of lushness that seemed to go on forever, but the program was conducted by a Dr. Walter Fihlo, Brazilian Professor of Ecology at England's University of Bradford. Probably a very small world (for all its size) actually exists out there! And even though I've never seen it, I heard I was on T.V. again! This makes the third time. If I leave nothing else on Dominica, I'll leave my image on video tape!

In my last letter I copied a few of my journal entries for your "amusement." I'd like to do that again and begin back on September 22.

September 22, 1993

After shopping I had lunch in Roseau today, followed by a big piece of chocolate cake! Every time I eat an excess of calories, along comes something to use them up! Sure enough when the transport passed Soufriere headed towards Scott's Head, we found the road closed. Rather than wait 'till 6:00 p.m., I chose to walk the remaining mile, loaded down with pack and sacks, to Scott's Head and up, up, up my hill! A young fisherman carried my day pack to the foot of the hill, a blessing! I'd never had made it drenched damp, damp body, sun hot! After putting groceries, et cetera, away, reading heavenly mail, and getting a bite to eat, I headed down the hill to the Scott's Head school for an ENCORE working group meeting that never materialized so joined the adult education committee instead. Home by 7:30, every single cake calorie used up!

September 24, 1993

Riding on the transport to work today in the soft morning light, I watched an orange and cream colored canoe resting calmly in the waters of Soufriere Bay as its sole occupant, a black man as weathered as his battered hat and tattered shirt, wound fishing line round and round a wooden reel, the silver blue sea stretching out behind him as far as I could see.

September 30, 1993

Last night we had another storm! I woke about 3:00 a.m., the whole house sounded like a thundering herd battering on the roof, beating at the windows, and coming through my open upstairs door. In fact, I got out of bed onto a <u>wet</u>, <u>wet</u> floor; came downstairs to get my torch (flashlight) and the radio. Electricity still on, closed all doors upstairs and tightened up windows I'd left ajar earlier. The sounds unsettled me enough that I decided to try the couch. Quieter on the ground floor, but couch uncomfortable so I tried downstairs bedroom. Bed was wet from wind-blown rain that made its way between the covers. My only option lay back upstairs. By this time I'd sort of gotten used to the sounds: rain pelting the galvanized roof and wind ripping down the mountainside bending each and every tree in its path! Waking up about 7:00 a.m. – all quiet! Only lost one tree in back yard, more from rain, I'm sure, than wind.

October 1, 1993

I spent Saturday and Sunday with Mary Peterson. I'd forgotten what an adventure riding over to the Carib Territory can actually be! The transport picked me up in Roseau on Saturday about 8:00 a.m. The driver, Bogart, had already been up way before dawn to pick up a group of workers in the small village of Bioche on the westward side of the island and taken them to the Carib Territory to work on a church. "Someone" had failed to deliver materials on Friday to the work site so Bogart got the job! After a stop at the supply yard and the gas station, we had two 2x6s, 14-feet long laid along the transport's seatbacks from the open back to the front window. Underneath the seats, stacked side by side in stacks of three, lay six 12-foot 2x6s that Bogart weighted down with a sack full of sand. Three 1x8s also under the seats and tilted on edge, clung to the side door wedged in by the door and a 25 gallon drum of diesel fuel.

Once loaded, away we went over the winding climbing road from Roseau across the island's high peaked center, through clouds, fog and drizzle, down, down, down to the Atlantic and the 3,700 acre Carib Reserve. Young Caribs unloaded the transport, stacking two long heavy boards across one shoulder and marching up winding concrete steps to the top of a hill overlooking the sea. One young man even balanced his boards across his shoulder and walked up the steps while his hands hung loosely at his sides. (They're building a Church of Nazarene.)

Transports are mini-vans, often Toyotas that hold 1-15 people. I've seen them crammed with about 25 children! Passengers enter by a sliding side door. The back opens up and out to accommodate baggage behind the last seat, or, in this case, so the lumber could hang out. And guess where all the exhaust fumes went? Directly up, hit the raised back door, were swept into and through the van, being captured and held at the front window. By the time we got to the Territory, did our eyes ever burn! The ride can take anywhere from an hour to an hour and one-half. This time Bogart made it in less than an hour!!

October 19, 1993

ENCORE Dominica has a technical officer, Michelete, due in today from Haiti where he worked for W.W.F. (World Wide Fund for Nature). But Air France wouldn't let him and his family board the plane! "ENCORE's contract is only with you," officials told Michelete, "not with your family!" (Note: About a week later Michelete, his family and all their household belongings did make it out of Haiti. But things got pretty tense for a while.)

October 20, 1993

Today after work, as I walked from the office to return the keys to the watchman Mr. Devernay, I spied a bright red substance running down a small open drain which divided a long concrete slab that I had to cross to reach Mr. Devernay's small wooden hut situated at the rear of a much larger block house. I pondered; dye? But it looked suspiciously like fresh blood! Sure enough, once I reached the back yard I came upon four men sitting in an open shed, talking away while a dead pig lay stretched out on the concrete, throat slit, everything still in place including the head, bright red blood making its way across the slab into the small open drain where it traveled on its way to the village road. "Yes," answered the men to my query, they'd just killed the pig, were letting it bleed out, would butcher soon and share meat between them. (In the same spot, not many days later, I startled a lady who squatted on a small wooden stool scrubbing what appeared to be a stomach lining. This time, instead of a pig the dead animal looked like a dog, head intact but attached to a decidedly hair-covered hide while its insides unceremoniously littered the slab at the lady's feet. This time my stomach lurched!

October 23, 1993

I got my first mail today after almost two weeks. Eleven letters! My feelings hard to explain. First, my joy in reading each and every word, not only for its beauty being written by a friend/dear one, but the thoughts, feeling of support they convey; news from home, how everyone is coping with their own lives; and the incredible insights into my life, movements, the caring for my experience to be a good, satisfactory one! It is overwhelming how blessed I feel after reading each and every letter!

October 29, 1993

It's Creole Day. I'm working at home. Plan to dress in my national wear (white blouse and gathered with bright red ycllow, and green bows), watch the Scott's Head school's Creole Day program, then return home to work on my October report and begin a grant proposal to help the SHIC build benches and place garbage containers along Tuo Sab Beach and at the top of Point Cachacrou. Cachacrou in Carib means "That which is being eaten away." The proposal, an SPA (Small Project Assistance) grant, is funded by USAID but through Peace Corps, not ENCORE. It seems like everything is connected!

End of Journal

Continuation of letter dated Nov. 14, 1993

It seems, at this point, I live from day to day where if I don't write them down, images and details are wiped out of my mind by what happens next. Just recently I pulled quite a cultural booboo! Can you imagine after being here 16 month? The mess-up wouldn't have been so bad by itself, but the timing blew everything out of proportion. I'm now a much humbler PCV than I was a month ago.

Next week there's an all-volunteer conference where I hope enough cross cultural training goes on that I can stay out of the "minefield" from now on. I really think my biggest problem is I stopped walking on eggs. But only for a short while. I've met a spiritual prophet who brings me limes, avocado pears, soursop and bay leaves!

Its answers like the following gone given in response to my question, "How long does it take to get to Grand Bay when you walk on the track?" That is so Dominican. "If you're accustomed to walking and its walk you're walking; one day you'll reach!"

Well, dear friends and loved ones, I think of you all so often. Your letters are so very special. Thank you.

Love, Mary Ann

P.S. You'll be proud of me; I'm co-existing with Mr. Spider! One morning as I opened the dish cupboard door, a big "wolf" spider scurried around the plates. I grabbed a cereal bowl and decided to leave the door open all day so the light would bother him and he might seek other shelter. Sure enough, the following morning he'd attached himself to the outside of the water pail sitting on the kitchen counter. My movements startled him into finding higher ground, and away he sailed to the food cupboard which I noticed he gained access to through the cracks between the doors and the frame. Much later he appeared in the hall corner just above the back door where he "hung out" for the rest of the day. Before going to bed that night, I mentioned that it would be an excellent idea if he were to go outside. Absolutely no sight of him since!

November 17, 1993

Dear Mom and Bill:

I received your card from New York! Sounds like you had a great time. Then I heard from Auntie Carol who said she and Patty did car bit to the airport. Then, I'm sure you heard I actually talked to everyone on the phone: Carol, Janet, Patty, Billie and Marshall. What a day that was. Also, because I'd just gone to airport (Canefield) to meet Lisa, a good friend of my niece Dawn who was in St. Martin when she called to see if she could come over to Dominica and stay. I'm not sure yet if it was a good idea. I've had some of the same reactions that I had when you and Bill took me on your ship The Festival! Plus, she's very young and I feel she misled me a little, but maybe not on purpose. I'll figure it all out after she leaves and write to Kathryn about the experience. Kathryn can share with you if she wants to.

My General letter, enclosed, should catch you up on me. I wrote it this past Sunday and finished printing it out today. Lot of work, but I sure do enjoy putting it all together. I'm pretty lucky to have an audience and the marvelous help at your end. I keep hoping I'll get to do them on a computer soon. But the Peace Corp one keeps breaking down and the ENCORE promised a laptop just isn't forthcoming.

I finally got over my latest setback: flu and all, so I'm in a pretty good mental and physical shape right now. I do like being here when that happens. Sure wish it could last for longer periods. Tell everyone hello. Happy Thanksgiving. I bet the turkey will (did) taste good.

Love, Mary Ann

February 5, 1994

Dear Mom and Bill:

I did it! My last General Letter! I'm saying my last because I'm hoping to be busy for the remainder of the time – the way I write these General Letters, they take mucho time! Oh, for the days at the computer. In fact, I was hoping to do this one on a computer and send it to you all typed. But no such luck.

Let's see if I have any directions for this letter (enclosed General Letter): Fourth line in second paragraph on page 1 should read: Mary Peterson's to the sound of a Carib Indian band…

When you do the journal entries just put a line or even an *. I decided it would be better not to date them since it is getting to be so long ago now!

Sorry about all the inserts, corrections, and arrows, et cetera! Like I mentioned in the note on page 14, if you have room or don't think it's too much, insert pages 17, 18, 19 and 20 at that spot as a continuation of my journal entry for the Portsmouth trip. Maybe since this is the last one, I won't hurt to pay a little more in postage – that is, if your typing fingers hold out!

I do get a kick out of putting them (it), the General Letters, together but I only expect you to do what is feasible. Thank you for words of encouragement for my writing. I love Auntie Carol telling me she has friends who want to meet me!

I'm very prolific this weekend and have also sent you off a Happy Anniversary card. I received Bill's letter last week and one from each of you a few weeks back. I finally got Kathryn and Caroline's Santa Claus Xmas card. It is really great. They look like two good looking ladies. Caroline looks so good. I just know all will be well with her.

As you already know, I got pretty excited when you told me I could rent your place if it worked out. I'm still excited. As I wrote either Caroline or Kathryn, I'm not sure what the draw is, but it seems to be there. Also, I understand my own renters may not be ready to buy a house in Auburn for another few years. Of course, living in the country means a car! Already worrying about economics!

It was so nice to hear from Bill and learn you are "just fine" again! I like to hear that. I'm believing 1994 is a good year. I can feel it in the air. Thank you for writing. I enjoyed that. Although, I'll have to admit when I saw the envelope I became excited about reading one of Mom's letter which I do enjoy so very much. Everyone who writes shares something different with me and almost always a part of themselves. So I like getting to know the both of you in a different way than I have before.

I remember her saying once, that the best thing for Lori and I was when she moved to Oregon. Of course, in that case she never wrote either, but I visited her on her home turf!

Caroline and Kathryn wrote all about Janie's visit. I enjoyed every word of their tales. I also received Ramona's journal of Scotland. I was able to read it all in one swoop while I waited for Bill to hike to Boiling Lake and back. Bill's trip was quite successful, for him and me. I've written Caroline and Kathryn details that I'm sure they'll share. Also, I took some photos which I'm sending to Bill who will eventually see that you all get them.

All of the things from Janie did come airmail and didn't cost much at all -- $3.29! I loved the her journal and the new calendar!

I'm reading a new health book that Bill Thomson brought: The McDougall Program. So far I'm interested. It would be hard to start the program here if I do exactly like he says – but I hope to come home close to a vegetarian. Can you be close to one?

Bill also brought: dried fruits, soup mixes, mixes for noodles, et cetera, and Bufferin! If I try the McDougal Program, maybe I can toss the Bufferin. Wouldn't that be a good deal!

Since my comments on "thinking desert," I've received book lists on desert themes, photographs of desert scenes and ideas! Even met a lady who's from Taos, New Mexico! There is still nothing that can't wait until after I get home. But you know me, it's the idea stage I like the best. The better for fantasizing!

My vacation (at home) was really good. I think I may have finally learned how to relax and hopefully maybe the ENCORE problems won't bother me! The higher-ups, meaning David Edwards (Dominica P.C. Program Director whom you met) has decided not to request volunteers to replace us. So far the ENCORE people don't know that. I hope its ok when they find out. It's all so sad because if someone (we are never allowed to) would get their act together, the whole thing could be an ideal setting for varied Peace Corps projects. If all four of us ENCORE Peace Corps didn't feel the same way, I might think it was my "workaholic" opinion. But just ain't so!

Bill, I just never wrote much more about Dominica sports. You'll have to quiz me when I get home. When Bill Thomson was here and went on his Boiling Lake hike – the trailhead was at the village of Laudat which we reached by going partway to Trafalgar (where you went when you were here). The following day, we drove to see the Trafalgar Falls and were they beautiful. It rained a lot just like when you were here, but the clouds would clear periodically and made everything sparkle, like it has a way of doing on Dominica. In fact, I guess you both came at about the same time Bill came – less than a month later. So climate and all pretty much the same.

I didn't take him to the Callalou to eat, but instead we went to the La Robe. It wasn't very good. I sure can't figure out why I always have such good meals and when I bring company something happens! Even when I took Lori, Caroline and boys to my favorite Orchard House, the hamburgers weren't as tasty as usual! Oh, well!

Shall close now! Thanks for the big job you are about to do!

Love, Mary Ann

February 5, 1994

Dear Family and Friends:

It's a beautiful day in Scott's Head, Dominica: varied gray overcast clouds, a patch of blue here and there, rain showers, coolness, breezy, very little humidity (that I can feel), exactly like it's been almost every day since November. I feel I'm getting spoiled, having forgotten what the truly hot weather is like! But I do remember last February when the sun finally decided to show itself for hours at a time! I know that now under these cloudy skies the suns moving ever northward on the horizon and will soon be directly overhead, leaving no shadows to escape from the heat! But for now, I'll enjoy!

I have this sense of time fleeting, yet I enjoyed a long, slow month of vacation by passing the

Christmas holiday in Portsmouth, welcoming in the New Year at Mary Peterson's, to the sound of a Caribbean Indian band, reading, writing, visiting, sleeping late, and gaining weight. Then finally during the last week of January, happily enjoying and entertaining company from the United States! Actually, Dominica entertained Bill Thomson who fully enjoyed his short seven-day visit while driving all over the island's winding narrow bumpy road in a small, four-wheel drive, red, foreign Jeep, on the left-hand side of the road!

Wouldn't you think this time I'd offer to drive and let my company gawk? No! But you should have heard me complain when Bill drove too close to the edge of a cliff! You'll have to get Bill's opinion first-hand, but the highlight of his trip (besides the Atlantic's crashing waves) may have been his five-hour trek to Boiling Lake in the wind and the rain. Claimed to be a six-hour hike (three hours in and three hours out), Bill and his guide made it, elevation gain and all, in 2 ½ hours in and 2 ½ hours out! The trailhead at the village of Laudat shows on the map at 1,750 feet. From there it is ups and downs to the bubbling lake, across the 3,000 foot slopes of Morne Nicholls! Needless to say, I found it hard to return to "work"!

While ENCORE's still out of funds with no relief in sight, I've received a small assistance grant from USAID for Scot's Head Beach Enhancement: benches, garbage containers, and a new sign. I wrote the project in conjunction with the Scott's Head Improvement Committee and we'll start work after Carnival. Carnival in Dominica (February 14 and 15 this year) take priority over every-thing! I'm excited about the project.

A very special part of my Christmas holiday included all of your cards, gifts, and letters. I can say no more than "Thank you"! You all continue to be so special to me. For the remainder of this letter I'm resorting to undated journal entries, hoping they convey some of my thoughts, activities and feelings over the past few months.

We took the Soufriere forms' students on a "plant walk" today. Mark took the boys. I took the girls. As we walked, the girls picked a grand assortment of leaves, flowers, and weeds, making all into a colorful bouquet. Then they marched down the middle of the road singing, "Here Comes the Bride"! One young lady asked me is my hair scratchy. I bent over and let her discover the answer for herself.

A close friend of Dawn Bachman (my niece) is staying here for a week. Anya, Dawn's friend, tells me she's found you learn your lessons much faster in the tropics! "It's all pretty intense!" She one whose actions can be (and almost always are) instantaneous! After a week's stay she left for parts unknown. I envied her freedom, but not the lessons she still had to learn.

As I walked from the bus stop to the office in Soufriere this rainy morning, Marfa (Mark's neighbor) called "Mary Ann. Mary Ann. Our waterfall. Look! Look!" Turning around to look up the valley where Marfa pointed I saw white water pouring long cascading streamers straight out of the jungle, down over the edge of the Soufriere Crater rim, down, down till they disappeared into their own spray and the valley's lushness. "The waterfall only comes after plenty of rain!" said a very proud and happy Marfa as I watched the breathtaking phenomenon, spellbound.

The Soufriere fishermen pulled two more sharks up on the beach today. "Probably caught," said Mr. Eli "by using a long line way out to sea in the channel." Sharks are numerous now. These are the fourth ones for Soufriere; Scott's Head fishermen catch them, too. Todays are large! One was 200-300 pounds, the other much bigger, at least the size of the fishermen's wooden canoes, "his" skin so thick and tough looking, almost like rough wood, but deep gray and discerningly pliable. I held back tears watching the big beautiful animal stretched out on the gravelly beach, a large rock placed in "his" mouth to keep the jaws open, one eye looking human staring up at me while fisherman sloshed "his" stark white insides with buckets of salt water to flush away the blood!

This morning while I got on the transport at Scott's Head, a fisherman carried a red plastic washtub full of cut up fish and an empty white plastic five gallon pail to the standing water pipe by the bus stop. Here he squatted, washing his large fish steaks under the running water – taking them first from the red tub, rinsing them and placing the rinsed ones in the white bucket. "What kind of fish, Tom?" I asked the transport driver. "Pretty large tuna, maybe," Tom replied. But then he asked a young school girl to shout out the window and inquire. "Shark," came back the answer. Tom speculated, "A small shark then, 200 pounds, maybe!" The steaks appeared to about three inches thick, a good foot across and equally as long! I'm told shark is mostly water. When cooked it boils down to almost nothing! Fish usually sells for $5.00 EC a pound in Scott's Head. But shark sells much, much cheaper!

I ate lunch today, Thanksgiving Day, standing on the back stoop of the Soufriere ENCORE office looking out toward the ridges of Soufriere's volcanic crater and surrounding jungled hills. My menu: Fried rice with chicken, sliced avocado pear, fried plantain and a peanut butter sandwich, all tasty, filling and easy to prepare. It didn't feel like Thanksgiving; no crispness in the air or falling leaves, no colors of oranges and yellows, dried grass or wheat-colored hills. No football games, family, babies, smells of turkey, dressing, cranberry sauce, browning rolls or pumpkin pie. No last-minute phone calls, "When should I be there?" No snores from the depths of the living room couch, grandchildren walks or sounds of young cousins playing. No trip planned or holiday for tomorrow! But tomorrow Peace Corps is hosting a buffet turkey dinner with all the trimmings! I can hardly wait!

Buffet dinner nice! Turkey, gravy, varied salads, vegetable trays, breadfruit and fish croquettes, rice, chocolate cake and pumpkin pie! Val went as my guest. We both ate very well! It was swallowed up by all the other volunteers or assertiveness of everyone around me including Val.

Riding the transport home to Scott's Head after dinner, I watched a sleek cruise ship operated by computerized sails, lit up from stem to stern and top to bottom, move slowly past Dominica. As lights from a full Caribbean moon glimmered on the ship and surrounding sea, I wondered if the passengers on the intricately designed vessel could see the moonlight all around them or even know how beautifully it must have outlined and illuminated the island paradise they came to see! I thought, too, of how I live in two worlds, maybe three, or maybe the edge of all, never truly belonging to any – the world of Peace Corps, the back home middle class world, and my own private volunteer life in a village.

While waiting for the transport today after work on my favorite rock wall in Soufriere, young, dark, uniformed boys ran down the street from school in the rain, laughing, shouting, sailing sticks in the open drain running full with water. Others walked in the same rushing drains in new white tennis shoes. I like the feel I get sitting on the rock wall, watching. A young, dark girl "lazes" on the corner; an old man, dressed in slacks, squats on his haunches; the bread van stops to sell fresh loaves to village women standing in the rain who have come down the street or out from nearby houses. The transport comes, I climb in over a gas cylinder, plastic bags full of groceries, duffel bags, school bags, to sit among uniformed children going home from school, women who've been to market or shopping in Roseau, and young men just "hitching" a ride rather than walking in the rain.

I usually share the short rock wall with other villagers, old women and men keeping track of the late afternoon activity. On another day, three naked boys who looked like brothers skipped up the road from the creek where they'd had a bath – the oldest leading the way, keeping the youngest out of the path of vehicles, as the "crazy lady" of Soufriere with her strange Creole chant, paced back and forth; her black plastic sandals unbuckled and mismatched, her tattered skirt and blouse hanging loosely on her thin body. Just as she made it to the middle of the road, a barefoot young boy rolling a bicycle rim by pushing it with a stick shouted, "Ho!" She turned around and crisply marched back to the edge of the road, her steps as precise as if they'd been choreographed, her voice sounding out her chant like a drill sergeant shouting cadence! The boy who called a halt to the "madwoman" never lost a roll on the bicycle rim or wavered from his path!

Four other youngsters came running down the hill in the middle of the road, I'm sure on their way to the stop to buy ice pops; smiling faces, money in hand, barefoot, boys in threadbare T-shirts and shorts, girls in worn skirts and blouses. Four men, maybe 18-22, "hung out" under the covered bus shed drinking beer, teasing the prettiest girls who happened by. The transport came, all too soon. Again, I climbed over cylinders, bags of groceries, boxes of beer, and a woman in a perky hat to the back seat. Everyone, it seems, had been Christmas shopping in Roseau. One heavy set woman stepped own off the bus in the middle of Soufriere with at least ten assorted boxes, bags and a gas cylinder, as she watched over her purchases like Mary's hen looks out for her chicks! Transports move extra fast now because there is more money to be made during these pre-Christmas days, horns honk louder and more often, people move at a brisker pace with a sense of purpose, something important to do! I love watching it all!

The day started out sunny and warm, then turned overcast and humid. It's just finished raining enough to fill my overflow barrel. The sky's a dull gray, while the sea reflects it back, actually looking cold! From my upstairs window I watch the constant turquoise water ripple over the coral reefs onto the sand. "Little" white caps lap upon the beach on both sides of the point (Atlantic and Caribbean) but hardly any can be seen out at sea. The water's "running" more like a huge lake or wide river today. As the sky to the southwest breaks, the color of silver shines on the sea at the far horizon, laid down by great shafts of light that slant downward. The shafts resemble inverted rain sheets from the softening clouds. The white caps pick up, especially in the bay. And it's hard to tell from here how dry the grass on the point really is because now it's only a dark shape etched against the blue-gray sea and sky.

Gusts of wind take the bayside palms which do not bend but give that impression because their branches sway, first one way and the other. The reverse sway is only in reaction to the lessening of the wind. This motion reminds me of great arms reaching out but unable to grasp whatever it is they are after. No other tree does quite this "dance" that the palms do. Where other trees are individual, the palms seem always in unison. It is only in the wind that they have a personality – otherwise they are "just there." Even their fruit hugs the trunk, growing in protected clusters away from where the fronds begin their reaching.

I'm sitting at the dining room table (dining room still seems a strange term to be using in the Peace Corps) soaking my foot in hot water, but since I used ice this morning (24 hours too late) maybe the hot temperature will compensate. Actually, I slipped, bending my big toes, yesterday morning while getting out of the shower. I felt the pain of it all, saw it was badly bruised, but dressed, put on my shoes and went off to work

During the day I felt tenderness whenever I bent my foot, but never bothered to take off the shoe and look. So last night the toe was quite swollen and an ugly purple-blue. But I felt sure by this morning it would look and feel better. Wrong! So here I am home from work soaking away with a 5:00 p.m. LSMT meeting to look forward to, but I don't think I can make it down the hill. Actually, between heat and ice, I've enjoyed staying home today: cooked a big pot of pink beans, washed clothes, wrote a long letter home, labeled a stack of slides and read!

The waves and white caps larger today than I've seen before. Strange for such a relatively calm day. Even the Atlantic side of the Point looks different. The waves break from a westerly direction and they've washed silt from the shore off into the sea, making it a light clayish color surrounded by turquoise. I speculated to my landlord that maybe it's an unusually high tide. He comments "Strange things can happen now! There's a new moon in the sky." Note: Val mentioned later when he drove me to the LSMT meeting that El Nino can cause rough seas in the Caribbean, and that each – usually around Thanksgiving – the sea gets very rough! This year the water washed way up to the Scott's Head/Soufriere road, causing considerable damage to those sections that the road crew had just repaired.

I'm teary today! On the way to the bus stop after work, Mark swoops up a young village child, lifting her high above his head. Age and homesickness catch me at the same time. I walk on, tears right on the surface. When the transport comes, its ever-present tape deck plays Christmas carols – country and western style – all the way to Scott's Head. No place to hide this time, so I swallow a lot! Today's Mark's first day back to work after a month's vacation of island hopping. He seems content and rested, professing happiness at being back on Dominica and in being lucky enough to be a PCV on this island!

While Mark was gone, his PCV roommate, Scott Duckett from Dexter, Oregon, flew to Washington, D.C., for foot surgery. But his bones were not healing properly, and the PC rule (of which there are so many) is that any medical emergency/situation not cleared up in 45 days requires that the PCV be medically separated. That's exactly what happened to Scott. So Dominican ECs are down to eight; the seven Ms, Mary, Marie, Mark, Melanie, Mike, Melissa, Mary Ann, and Charles!

It's Wednesday morning, day three of my vacation if I don't count Christmas Day and Boxing Day. I arrived home from Portsmouth about 4:00 p.m. yesterday. I'd been at Melanie's since Friday. She didn't feel well during most of my visit, but we did some fun things together anyway. Like a Sunday afternoon trip to Pennville in a pickup full of tipsy holiday merrymakers, and a Monday night dinner at the Purple Turtle Beach Resort, eating on the beach, watching the flickering lights of Prince Rupert's Bay's many sailing yachts.

I'd forgotten how long a 45-minute bus ride to Portsmouth can be. I loved seeing the island's west side with the trees starting to turn. The leaves seem brighter, more colorful this year – golden jewels among all the green. I imagine how intense the colors would seem to me if I'd lived on Dominica all my life. While Scott's Head's been dry and windy, Portsmouth's had lots of rain, generated by 4,747 foot Morne Diablotin.

I so enjoyed seeing Melanie in her tidy, compact home situated along a maze of concrete sidewalks and drains in the village of Lagoon just north of Portsmouth, real aluminum screens on all her windows. Melanie shares the place with PCV Todd Knight who'd gone home for Christmas, and KenRoy, now officially Melanie's boyfriend. It seemed as natural as can be to be a guest in their space where I used to get nervous and upset in Zicack when Melanie and I lived together if KenRoy didn't go home by 10:00 p.m.

Kenroy has always treated me with a great deal of respect. He says I'm like his mom. In fact, on Christmas night coming back from a walk to his uncle's rum shop in Zicack, Melanie, KenRoy and I stopped for chicken and chips at a small side street café where lots of holiday drinking and revelry were taking place. KenRoy tried to "protect" me from a Frenchman who desired to take me dancing at the marketplace. Refusing the persistent fellow's advances, I did give him my Scott's Head telephone number amid KenRoy's, "You'd better treat her with respect!"

Both Midnight mass and Sunday mass were all I remembered and more. On Christmas Eve, dressed in their familiar red skirts and white blouses, the choir sang from 11:00 to 12:00 on a raised platform in front of the congregation. Then, just before midnight Mr. John Alexis (chairmaster) announced they had to move outside and accompany Father "Reggie" down the aisle. About ten minutes later they came down the aisle, singing the entrance hymn, all decked out in brand new robes, oyster shell white, full-length cloth robes adorned with purple neck scarves. Mr. Alexis was dressed in blue and white satin.

During the two-hour service we sang every Christmas carol from "Silent Night" to "Hard the Herald Angels Sing" to "Come All Ye Faithful" to "Oh, Holy Night," my favorite. Even the congregation, ho usually sings out as loud as they can, tuned down to the choir's gentle harmonizing sounds, creating such a reverent atmosphere in that already holy church. Or, as Father "Reggie" chants, "You're standing on holy ground!" All so beautiful even amid the ritual of standing, kneeling, and of incense passing back and forth on the Father, the Altar, the Book, the Choir, and even the congregation. It must be the pageantry of it all that I'm taken with. Portsmouth mass is like a musical production every time I go.

After service on Sunday I started up the aisle looking for my old Zicack friend Walter who used to walk me home from church most every Sunday. And I saw him standing dark and tall at the back of the church in his accustomed spot, his black hair thick and shining, and his same off-white polyester suit not quite as tight as I remembered it, a scowl on his face, looking at me. As I approached him with my hands outstretched, the raised his in front of his face. "Don't talk to me!" he said. "You never told me you were moving to Scott's Head! Don't talk to me!" Of course, his defenses soon weakened and he wanted to know how long I was staying in Portsmouth before "he lost me again?"

At that moment I wish I can more than I do. I wish I can stay and talk for a long, long time. I wish to be close to this man in my conversation – something I know best, my comfort zone, and my familiar territory. But I can't. I do not know what to say other than, "How are you? Merry Christmas. I'm staying four day, but I'll be back before I return to the States in June." And I must leave the rest up to my spirit to let him know I care for him and count him a good friend. Somehow, even though his words are scarce and repeated over and over I think he knows. And I understand I'm also his friend.

This weekend, too, I walked through Zicack and Portsmouth, feeling like I'd not been gone for five months. People waved, smiled, spoke, kissed and hugged me. Children, like Loic and Pernella, came running from a block away, grasping me around the waist in a big hug saying, "Mary Ann, Mary Ann!" Miss Bess invited me in for Christmas wine. Lucky Lilly laid at my feet while I sat in the small cluttered living room where Miss Bess had painted walls and hung new curtains for Christmas. Miss Bess is the 70-year-old sister of our very first landlord, Earl; Lucky Lilly, the dog whose life we save. Miss Bess said Lucky Lilly had pups (her second litter). The next day, so did her sister. As the sisters' pups dropped, Lucky Lilly took them to <u>her</u> own nest. All that night and the next day sister whined and cried. Then as if to say, "Well, if you want them that much, you can have them all!" Lucky gave the whole brood to sister and never once nursed her own puppies again. Miss Bess says she walks around like a supervisor overseeing the whole operation. But from that day on, sister nursed them all

Fruitcake arrived today from England. During my holiday visit to Portsmouth, Mrs. Andre invited me to lunch with her family and guests from London. Following a scrumptious traditional Dominican holiday meal, one of her guests, Mr. Anthony, mentioned his wife and sent a homemade fruitcake for Mrs. Andre which he'd forgotten to bring along from Tibauld. (Tibauld being where he was staying on Dominica without his wife who was still in England.) He asked if there was any way he could send me a piece of his rum-soaked goody! Mrs. Andre said, "We have way." Sure enough, the cake arrived at Mrs. Andre's house from Tibauld where she gave Melanie a tightly wrapped piece of cake to give me. Four days later Melanie took it to an ENCORE meeting in Roseau (I'm still on leave) where she gave it to Val who three days later handed it to me as he passed by my house. Yummy!

(End of journal entries.)

The second "casualty" among the E.C. 59 PCV group was a woman named Liz from Seattle who went home last week because she's going to have a baby.

This letter seems to contain very little work-related news, probably because I'm on vacation. But one of the most satisfying activities that I work on continues to be the Environmental Education program. During December, after much arranging and organizing, I got to take 40 students from both schools (Scott's Head and Soufriere) and their teachers on a field trip to the historic Springfield

Plantation and Archibald Tropical Research Center. It turned out to be a bigger treat for the youngsters that I ever imagined.

Even though it's only February, this may be the last General Letter I send home. But I'll continue to look forward to seeing all of you and promise to answer anyone who writes to me. Do you know I'm considered "The Mail Queen?" I love it, and you!

Mary Ann

P. S. I have piped water! But in true Dominican fashion, all but one toilet and sink shutoff valves leak. Also, I discovered why West Indian women wear skits: To keep lizards from crawling up their pant legs. It was his tail I saw first, down below my knee, the rest of him hidden in the folds of my slacks. Now I roll them up, and that particular lizard lives under my fridge. And did you know lizards leave turds? One morning a caller had left quite a large dropping on my kitchen counter, about three times the size I'm used to wiping up. Later, while I was doing dishes, I think I saw the responsible fellow poised on the kitchen window. As I shooed him out so I could shut the window, he hissed at me. Someone mentioned that back in the States the bug man's standard line is, "if you have lots of spiders in your house that means you have lots of insects." Do you think my spider crop attracts larger lizards? Not to worry. Most of my spiders are only Daddy Longlegs, something I grew accustomed to as a tiny tot growing up on a farm.

February 26, 1994

Dear Mom and Bill:

After sitting for two and a half days at a workshop in firm plastic chairs, I'm sitting again!

But this time on one of my soft dining room chairs that cut off my circulation somewhere between my seat and back of my knees. The white plastic chairs stop the blood flow a little closer to the knee!

I learned such a good lesson, one I know you already know at the workshop (better known as an IST – In-Service Training) on Environmental Education. The lesson, "The older you get, the harder it is to take changes in lifestyle, i.e., food, eating time, bed rest, exercise habits and, in my case, even weather changes!"

Just like last year, the workshop was held at the Layou River hotel where it rained, the wind blew and it was cold! By Thursday night, between sitting and cold (remember it's all relative) I had a few aches and pains that the drier climate of Scott's Head had erased! The next changes included meals. We didn't eat until 7:30/8:00 at night a switch from my 5:30-6:00. Then the delicious food contained two meat dishes rice, salads, a bread, potatoes and dessert for both lunch and dinner! Of course eggs bacon and toast for breakfast. And I ate every meal! I simply have no will power when it comes to food! A number of the PCVs are vegetarians and they resisted, easily, all the fish, chicken, goat mutton, and pork chops! But not me, even though I've been on a fairly vegetarian/carbohydrate diet for a long while now. You can imagine the grumbling going on in my insides until new digestive inroads could materialize. And we won't even talk about salt!

Janie sent me a dried piece of desert sage. Does it smell good. Kathryn called before she went to the desert with Clive over President's Day. So my imagination is still being tempted. K.G. says no one seemed too happy with Janie's journal while she visited good old Auburn and environs, except Billie and Marshall. I've only received one issue, the one about Kayla's S'Top It. I can hear Kayla myself 'cause she's always talking in the background when Lori calls! Neither she nor Kyle will talk to me on the phone. Wonder if I'll get the same brush-off at home! No doubt! Times' been too long without Grandma. Although I do think Lori keeps me pretty alive to them.

Josh called last weekend he, Deb and I had a nice talk. I look at the photos Lori took while she was here quite regularly. They are nice!

My next workshop is COS in Nevis on March 23-25. COS stands for Close of Service. We'll learn more about P.C. paperwork for getting out! I hear it will be as bad as getting in was!

Hello to all.

Love, Mary Ann

March 20, 1994

Dear Mom and Dad:

It's Sunday morning, as you can tell from the date, tomorrow is the first day of spring. I'm waiting to get ready for mass, and have just finished my Sunday morning cooking. Today I cooked rice and veggies, ready to put together, and a yummy smelling spaghetti sauce! I've discovered an unsliced solid, small load wheat bread at one of the bakeries in town so I feel fairly healthy for now!

Mary Peterson, who has a working oven, has been baking her own wheat bread and cornbread. She'll call up and say, "I made fresh bread today!" I can almost smell it over the phone. The young lady (38) that I've met from Taos, New Mexico, Patricia, has discovered a bakery in Scott's Head behind one of the houses on the main street. Patricia, who is also an artist (watercolor you'd enjoy!) says the ovens are ancient like the 1800s! So I must go see it one day. She also says the bread is more like our French bread at home, not quite as doughy as the rest of Dominica bread. However, I've found a great deal of variety in the breads themselves as well as in the names: Erics, Sukies, Raffouls, Ruebans, and Golden Loaf. Bread can be found in slice white and wheat, small unsliced wheat loaves, and what I call "torpedo like" solid loaves of white or wheat in two or three sizes, from six inch to a foot. Everyone buys bread fresh daily because at least one bakery – Golden loaf – delivers every day but Sunday to bread depots in every village (I think) on the whole island! There's also a small square biscuit bread that comes hooked together.

I just went upstairs to bathe (shower). I've been taking my shower in late afternoon when I come home from work because now that I have "piped" water, it (the water) is almost always nice and warm by then. It (the pipe) runs all the way from Soufiere underground and all the way up to my hill in the hot afternoon sun! Solar heated water! But the morning – no such luck! It's been raining every morning for three days and this morning is no exception! So I had a cold shower! But not too bad. I actually feel quite refreshed. All during the "cold" weather (January mostly), I carried hot water upstairs to take warm showers. The cold just got too hard on the "ole back."

Bill Smith (from high school) who now lives in North Carolina, as you now, called last night.

Such a pleasure to talk to someone from home, well, actually that's not really home – but the tie with Placer County is still there. Can you imagine I've been out of high school 40 years? I've also heard from Walter Brown (Doc's son) in Bakersfield. He just recently lost his job (news director for a T.V. station in Bakersfield, I think). He's not worried and is kind of looking forward to the job search and a change of careers, maybe. Eva Brown is in a health care facility in Bakersfield. Still sharp as a tack, says Walter. But she cannot remember minute to minute, so must have care. She'll tell Walter every time he visits about my letter to her which Walter says she keeps on her dresser. I've written again.

Hope you are all in good health. Enjoy the spring.

Love, Mary Ann
P.S. It's really like fall here except for temp.

April 5, 1994; 8:00 p.m.

Dear Mom and Bill:

I'll start your letter on my birthday, or what's left of it. But I'll probably only get a little written. My eyelids are dropping and the arm, wrist and fingers are beginning to rebel! I've written two reports, a work calendar and a letter already today; just finished five journal pages and wrote almost all day yesterday! The shoulder, neck, arm and fingers got so stiff, sometimes I feel like a statue!

But it's been a filled, productive birthday. And you know how I like to produce! Kenroy just called and wished me happy birthday. That was fun. Melanie called earlier today at work. She told me that Kenroy's Dad was in Martinique for a week where he's playing with the Cultural Group from that island. Mr. Alexis plays the accordion in a Dominican jing ping band which is considered "old time music here. And there are very few jing ping bands left on the island. The Martinique Cultural Group is footing the whole bill for Mr. Alexis' band's trip to Martinique. The band consists of a boom-boom, a tambour, a shack-shack and accordion. I like the sound and it is fun to dance to in steps handed down from the English colonial days! Reminds me a little of Swiss polka, but only a little. (You probably heard one on your trip.)

I've been to Roseau today and then at work from 10:00 to 4:30. Then I walked out to Tuosab to see how the project is coming along. It's been a real thrill, the way the project has gone. When I say "project," I mean the SPA grant I've done with the Scott's Head Improvement Committee. The villagers that have worked on the benches and cleaning the beach and making the sign are so proud. It's one of the first times that people inside and outside of Scott's Head are saying good things about Scott's Head. I am so happy for them.

Learned today about new "messes" that Thomas Paul has gotten involved in in Portsmouth. I count my blessings daily that I moved down here. I feel sorry for Melanie and Todd and wonder if I'd have stayed, if I'd have been a better influence on Thomas or if it would still be as bad as it is up there. I remember in my "past lives" how my bosses used to tell me I was the conscience, and that I kept them in line! Guess I just didn't want to play that role anymore!

I also remember, real early on in my ENCORE days, when I ask the APCO our Peace Corps ("boss") when does one draw the line between acceptable behavior in a professional setting on

Dominica and in your own bosses' private life. David Edwards (you met him. He is the APC who is also Dominican) told me that Thomas Paul's private life was no concern of mine unless it interfered with the job. It finally did and has continued doing so even before I asked to be transferred.

Boy, I hadn't thought about that in a long time. Well, I'll write more later, like tomorrow. But first Kathryn just called. What a special, special treat! Later!

April 6, 1994; 10:00 a.m.

Hi again!

I'm sitting outside the ENCORE office in Soufriere – locked out! This happens regularly. Sometimes I get upset, sometimes I don't. Today I'm upset. I've been up since 5:45 and on the bus to Roseau by 7:20. I was back in Soufriere by 8:50 having bought some plastic garbage bags for our project and tried to change an order for ten bags of cement to seven bags.

The cement business is probably why I'm mad rather than being locked out. But the key business for the ENCORE office has always been a pain. But it doesn't need to be because a watchman always keeps the key. And every time we leave and lock up, we are supposed to leave the key with the watchman, Mr. Devernay. However, our boss, Val, often goes with the key, meaning he locks up and takes the key home with him. And so he did this last night and has not showed up for work yet this a.m. – so here I am!

Mark's gone on to Roseau, being a male he refuses to wait around. I have thoughts of just going home, but decide to write you some more first. The cement business that set e off today involved the SHIC Beach project, also. Yesterday I traveled to Roseau to buy ten bags of cement. The yard was out of cement but expected a delivery by afternoon. So I paid for ten bags and the transport driver said he would pick it up in the afternoon.

But he didn't pick it up – and last night one of the men working on the project came by and said a local restaurant man had donated three bags of cement so I should only buy seven. So this a.m. I go to try and change the order and got "snapped" at! So I "snapped" back! But ended up just leaving the order for ten bags which the transport driver still hasn't picked up!

I'm now writing in the office. Val came about 10:30, all apologetic. He'd forgotten he'd gone with the key until he heard it rattling on the floor of the truck! Oh, well – life in the E.C.! I'm getting so good at going with the flow because everything eventually works out: always for the best. But every now and then something – like the lady "snapping" at me sets me off!

More later! By the way, I could use some dollars for the project – any little amount will do if you are so inclined. If you're not, that's fine, too. You've certainly more than already supported me 500%!

4:00 p.m.

A long day, hot one too, in the office. I'm ready to head home. Dread walking up my hill in the sun! Did I tell you my landlord is quite ill? I'm upset about that because I feel so helpless! He's had a major stroke then caught pneumonia in the hospital. His children are due to fly in from England today. I lit a candle in church for him on Easter Sunday. When I visited him I hospital on Saturday, he seemed resigned to his fate which upset me further. But then when I came home I realized he was totally paralyzed on the right side and how depressing that must be to him! I could not understand a word he spoke. His daughter-in-law had to interpret for me.

5:30 p.m. at home

I made it up the hill! Not as bad as I imagined; plus, I did project business on the way. Cement has been delivered. I gave plaster bags to Mr. Corbette (the man building the bench) and talked to Mrs. Detouche (the SHIC president about the project). Also found out Mr. Eli, my landlord, is better today.

I want to finish this rambling letter before I go upstairs to take a warm shower! I'm recycling Kathryn's hearts. They are such fun!

Your birthday card was lovely. Thank you. The photo of you both and Pam looks cold! Thank you for sharing. I don't think you look old at all. I have the volunteer heart of my fridge. It's "priceless"! Where did you find it? In Antigua I bought some black beans. Mary P. tells me they are good to substitute for meat in any Mexican-type dish. Haven't tried them yet. Bill, I enjoy your notes. I heard on the radio that baseball season opened (officially) in the States.

The young boys and young men now play lots of cricket in the street these past few weeks. Almost like the basketball has been exchanged for a cricket bat. They seem to use anything for their ball. I love the way they wind up/run/and throw the ball! I'm glad you explained "Scratch Head, Hair Turn Gray." I'm sure you are right! I'm not good at those things. But it didn't bother me because I don't get most of the Dominican proverbs, jokes, et cetera!

Have two letters from you both – March 5 and March 17. Glad Redwood City elder hostel was a good experience and even gladder you survived driving! I didn't know Pete Hawkins died. Kathryn B. also told me of Bunny Nakagawa. Enjoyed hearing of the baby shower. I wonder while I'm writing here if the baby's been born yet. Debbi sent me a photo of her and Bill. She does look young! You talk of your children turning 50 and 60. What about 40-year-old grandchildren?

I'm thoroughly enjoying my last weeks, days, months. In fact, my feelings are such that I now feel the experience has been quite positive. Can you imagine me saying that after some of my words earlier in the two-year assignment? Really enjoyed my vacation in St. Kitts and Antigua.

Take care, Love M.A.

April 24, 1994

Dear Mom and Bill:

Your notes and letters arrived Friday, one with photo and one with typed account of Pennville trip. You were right on the decision to leave it out of my General letter – it didn't even seem interesting to me and it was really a fun trip! Just goes to show you! Thank you for typing.

Thanks for the photo that Jamie and Jeannine took off of your deck. I believe my homeland is going to take some getting used to. I just hope I'm not completely let down like I was when I got off the plane in St. Lucia in July of 1992! I never felt that way at all about Dominica, but boy, was I ever disappointed in St. Lucia. Maybe it was good to land there first then Dominica looked all the better. I also remember how I despised Portsmouth the first time I went there, and it grew and grew and grew on me! It's like one (I) can find beauty in most anything – given a chance to adjust. I am wondering how big the mountains are going to look after becoming accustomed to Dominica's peaks and feeling they are huge!

The "girls" all called one night from Janice's. What a treat. I got the biggest kick out of Doug going off to haul a bull to Montana. Also, good to hear of Diane's new job. The "girls" sounded like they were having a wonderful time! I now have all these offers to stay a while in Oregon. They sound very interesting.

I'm imaging that by the time you receive this letter, Jeannine will be a mom and you'll be a grandma again! I wonder (did Jeannine tell Joyce what the baby was before he/she was born?) That could have been hard on Joyce knowing she didn't know!

Yes, you are also right about I've gotten to see some islands, not just Dominica. I've been pleased about that considering I didn't really have much of a desire to travel. But I find, this year as with last, after a while I get "cabin" fever. And it is so nice to be completely away because I could totally relax, something that is hard to do on your own island. It does get easier and easier to do as the time goes by at it's (as you say) lightning speed!

Bill, I spent a good hour last week learning all about cricket! I must say I could now enjoy watching a match/game. I get very curious often the player from Trinidad hit or got 375 runs before he "went down." It is really a fascinating game – something I never thought before having it explained to me. The young boys (and not so young) put up their wickets in the middle of the road on Scott's Head's main street and bowl away. Even the transports must dodge cricket players! I can keep my note, if you'd like and explain all when I return home. Of course, you may already understand it or not have any desire to hear about it. Both of which I would understand! Keegan, Melanie's old boyfriend, and the young man I introduced you to in Astaphans store the day you were here is the one who explained it all to me. I hope soon to also watch Keegan play in a tennis match. They start again in May he told me. Also hope your "squamous cells" came off all right!

You talk about signing up for an elder hostel in July in New York. Now there would have been a plan – I could have flown where you were finishing your trip and come home with you. But, I keep forgetting the cost! I'm working down to budgeting down to last pennies. I'll only get paid once more – on the first of May. This will include May through the 9th of June and have to cover rent, phone, electricity and gas if I need it, plus food and getting ready to come home. It all feels a little scary to me, and three of us have planned to rent a car next weekend to go around the island and take photos. I want to get more slides, even though the fall light is no longer here! I also have to buy short-term health insurance to carry me over until I get a job! But it will all work out as it always has. I've often said you have to be a little well off to join the Peace Corps. I believe it more and more. I'm one of the few PCVs on our island that lives on their pay. Well, almost – I've been known to charge on my BofA card!

The COS meeting in Nevis was real helpful. Besides getting my PC certificate, we had workshops on adjusting back in the Sates, how to fill out federal forms for jobs, a rehash of our PCV experience, how to look for jobs, and a little session on life planning. The life planning session was my favorite and I came away with the following gems:

Follow your heart

Provide structure

Tell yourself: I'm able to do this

It's okay to do this

It's not for the rest of my life

The "gems" were given in context of thinking about where we'd like to work next, what kind of a job. Another words don't limit ourselves in the planning stage. And most importantly, don't be too hard on ourselves. Actually a good lesson just for living!

I've done some pretty amazing things lately like seeing historical places on the island, written my DOS (Document of Service), started my medical procedure to "get out of here" and worked diligently on the SPA project which is turning out to be something and is getting talked about all over Dominica. I hope I don't jinx it by saying that! But I'm now happy with my "contribution" to the island and that is such a plus!

Mom, please accept this letter as a Happy Mother's Day greeting. It is meant in the sincerest of terms with love and best wishes.

Love, Mary Ann

May 8, 1994

Dear Mom and Bill:

So you'll know (ten days from now) that even though I don't call today, I am thinking of you. Such a Mother's Day it is in Scott's Head. Mothers are honored at church all around the island. Everyone gets a new dress! It's a very special day.

In Scott's Head members of the youth choir met all mothers at the door to pin on them a small tag adorned with a gold ribbon. The tag simply said "Mother." But at the back they'd printed a number. During the service then, the choir had a drawing. The gifts all wrapped in shiny foil paper were handed out to some very happy women.

But I don't think anyone could have been prouder than or happier than me. It seems the Scott's Head Improvement Committee all got together and decided this would be a good day to say thank you to me. So: The Parliamentary representative, Mr. Maynard Charles who is also the Minister of Tourism and Trade, gave me a thank you speech. He told how I "mothered" the project and the village of Scott's Head. Next I got a beautiful bouquet of flowers, a gift and a card all the while, of course, tears streaming down my face. Not enough? The choir sang me a special song: Words enclosed. When I got home with gift and flowers, the gift turned out to be a coffee mug with my photo on it! The card said: "To a very nice Mother whom we know we will miss very much. We want to take the place of your children today. Have a very Happy Day and thanks for all your good works." It was signed by each member of the SHIC. I must say I feel about 100 feet tall!

I know you had a special Mom's Day, too. Mrs. Doutouch, the president of the SHIC and now chairwoman of the Scott's Head/Soufriere/Galleon Village Council (I run around with the right people), said I had more children than anyone for today: 900 from Scott's Head and 1,000 from Soufriere! Soon I'll get home and be just another average person! Think I can handle that?

We've had a strike scare and volcano scare since I last wrote. I think I wrote home about them and maybe you even saw it all on CNN. I was on T.V. again. This time at the inauguration of the Village Council – a very fancy affair held at the Scott's Head School with government dignitaries and all!

I'm counting off the days on my calendar – today is day 35! Haven't heard if you're a great-grandma again or not. Just figure you are.

Made split pea soup again this a.m. I sure do like that stuff!

Take care. Hi to all. Love, MA.

May 22, 1994; 9:30 A.M.

Dear Mom and Bill:

Your statement, "Well, yours to enjoy, it being all a part of the Peace Corps experience," hit a very responsive chord.

I keep saying this will be my last letter, but here I write another one. So I'll say it again, this will probably be my last letter. I'm sitting on the back porch where the May sun no longer hits during the day having moved further north in the sky. The wind keeps rain at bay and has even blown away most of this morning's heavy grey clouds.

Three locals argue loudly in Creole just up the road from my house as they stand under a row of huge mango trees. I have no idea if they are arguing about the fruit hanging on the trees, the fruit the wind has knocked off – or something far removed from the mangoes. In fact, it's only their tone of voice which leads me to think they are arguing. That is not always the case given the loudness and aggressiveness of the locals anyway. I do regret not having learned Patois. But I seemed incapable. Some called it a mental block and this may be entirely true.

A young boy, son of the ENCORE office cleaning lady, fixed me up some cashews the other day. They are tasty. He had to go to the bush and pick them, roast them and shell them. They are such an interesting, pretty fruit when growing. The nut itself hangs down like a claw from the fruit. It also has a hard skin (shell) while the fruit is soft and edible as it hangs: The fruit is actually longer in relationship to the cashew nut than I have drawn. Fruit may be two to three inches, nut one a half inches. On some trees the mature fruit is bright waxy red, on others bright waxy yellow. The nuts are always dull grey. After nuts are picked, they must then be roasted.

I've seen this done once by some young boys last weekend on the beach in Portsmouth. They lit a fire in the sand from coconut husks, old wood scrapes and all – even got some charcoal somewhere. They placed a few rocks around their fire, enough to hold a three by two piece of tin on top of them. On top of the tin is where the cashew nuts went and stayed until they got black. The boys stirred or shook the roasting cashews now and again, but not too often. It is evidently the oil in the nuts which burns and blackens. I'm told this is an outside job! Not one for a cast iron fry pan over the stove in the kitchen. Once the nuts are roasted they are scooped into a can and then cooled.

The days are going by very fast. But I find each one a long way from June 10th. I've not had the feeling of euphoria and desire to stay on Dominica since the middle of April. This is a three-day holiday with tomorrow, Monday, being a beach party at TouSab. Yesterday we cleaned the beach and all, because the beach party is a fund raiser being put on by the SHIC. So today, I'm a little stiff! Tomorrow I'll "tend" bar!

Next weekend we have a going-away picnic at a special place on the northeast coast, and I'll spend the rest of the weekend with Mary – my last time to go see my favorite spot in the Atlantic. Then June 4 and 5 are reserved for packing. I've already given a lot of stuff away and also tossed yards of paperwork! During the week, ENCORE has picked up a little because we now have money again for a short while, and WWF has given the local site offices computers!

They are pretty nice, very powerful and loaded with all kinds of programs. I feel fortunate because now I can go home not quite as computer illiterate as I felt I'd become. Sure would have been great to have this one (and its laser printer) for all my general letters. Maybe I'd have written more! Ha. Ha! I've told everyone in the world how you are typing those letters and mailing them and all this has meant to me over the past two years. I hope I've mentioned it enough to you. Thank you so much.

Hope you found Billie and Marshall okay. I talked to them just at the end of April. Also will send Uncle M a birthday card. I sent Billie one but she'd not received it when they called the day before her birthday.

A watchman and gardener up the road on the big Bellot estate brought me by a whole bag of cherries on Friday night. So I made juice yesterday evening. I also tried to make jelly, but no such luck! The cherry juice is one of my favorites. The cherries look like those in U.S. but taste nowhere near the same. These are tart! Have two seeds inside and I find them hard to eat just plain. Where they look like you'd just want to devour them. The locals eat them off the tree like I would at home. What they do have in common with U.S. cherries is the birds absolutely love them, and they spoil in the brownish way that our cherries do.

Well, must shower and go to church! Nothing at all in Scott's Head like Father Reggie's service!

Love ya, M.A.
P.S. Thanks for last card. Nice painting!

August 26, 1995 – Garden Bar Road, Lincoln, CA

Written upon my return to the US

Dear Mom:

Since I don't have to mail you a rent check this month, the least I can do is write you a letter. (Again, thank you for your caring. It's been a blessing.)

I sent my inquiry off to Agri-Times Northwest or Northwest Agri-Times this morning. I discovered I'd mailed them my check on July 2nd. They had cashed it July 3rd. Wonder where the paper is.

This morning I talked to Nancy Crouch. She's been back in Cottonwood for almost two weeks and is delighted to be home. However, she says there is no one to talk with about what she's going through – at least no one who truly understands, and that makes it a little rough. Evidently in Tucson she was part of a bone marrow support group.

Her condition is stable, meaning her red and white blood count has stabilized, and she no longer requires weekly transfusions. Nurses come to the house every two days to draw blood so she is well monitored on that level. It will be at least a year before her immune system is functioning again, so she must take daily medication to prevent infection/disease. She'll continue to take steroids for at least another three to four months and has developed hairline fractures/osteoporosis due to the steroids and other medication. The doctors have recommended she use a walker. But she finds it very hard, ego-wise, to do so in public.

Nancy told me that before her surgery she had visions of coming back home and being able to go on hikes, continue her dance lessons, basically lead a pretty normal life. Now, of course, she realizes that's impossible and is having to come to terms with all the emotions and grieving her disappointment entails. To put it mildly, I'd not change places with her in a million years. Thank heaven for my small aches and pains.

Did I tell you I talked with Bob Morrelli the other day? He always asks about you and the rest of the family. If you remember, he got hit by a car when he was resting alongside the road and was pretty well banged up! One of his legs didn't heal properly and the doctors had to operate on it again this past service trip on the Pacific Crest Trail in the Trinity Alps where he'd hiked in for nine miles with a 60-pound backpack, then did trail maintenance for the next five days and hiked out again. "Much rougher" than he ever expected. He's trying to come to grips with the body pain that the accident left with him. Some days are better than others, I guess.

From the looks of the weather map, Kathryn and Caroline are having clear skies over on the coast. That will make for a nice vacation at Fort Bragg for Kathryn, so glad.

If I sound strange on the telephone lately, it is because I find that I don't care to talk on the telephone like I used to. It seems there is not enough time to truly "communicate," and if a problem or misunderstanding arises, it's hard to take the time to figure out what the other person is really saying. Plus, I hate being questioned, a habit I acquired on Dominica, probably connected with so much Peace Corps gossip. I find I get very uncomfortable and tend to clam up when I'm questioned, even though I often use this conversational tactic myself, especially when the other person isn't too communicative.

The Lincoln High School/Western Placer reunion is tonight. I'll attend, but haven't heard of too many of my friends who plan to do the same. Joyce and Jimmy are going to Karrie Wilson's wedding. I gather it's being held at John Wilson's, in the yard. Joyce tells me Karrie is marrying one of the Godley's. As Caroline says, "What a small world."

The figs are finally starting to ripen. I think I just hadn't been giving the tree enough water, well in the right places, that is. I'd water it with a small sprinkler at the base of the tree but I believe it needed water all over and lots of it! The persimmons, on the other hand, keep dropping off, but those that do stay are filling out.

Getting ready to go to Sedona keeps me extremely busy. There seems so many things to get ready at the last minute, and other things like the yard get left by the wayside. I've been trying to mow the lawn since Thursday night and it has not been mowed yet. I didn't get home until 5:30 Thursday. On Friday I came home at 5:00 but could barely make supper. I was so tired. Plus, I'd developed a kink in my shoulder from using the typewriter all morning on Thursday and stuffing envelopes on Friday. Then the mower developed another flat tire (its third one). Jimmy was to fix it this morning and bring the mower back down, but that didn't happen either. He fixed the flat, but the lawn mower is still up at this house. Maybe tomorrow!

I'm enclosing a little piece I wrote the other morning. Have an enjoyable fall!

Love, Mary Ann

The Old Garden Spot

I water this morning after my stretches and daily lesson at 6:30. Change the sprinkler on the lawn, move it from the falling, fruit laden fig tree to the stately persimmon. Figs won't ripen, persimmons drop. Walking around the corner of the garage I see the sun watching me as it comes up over the knoll behind the house. As the sun lights up the old garden spot a longing comes inside me. A feeling for something unknown, wanted, coupled with this spot and a place in Wallowa County: an early morning, sun rising and me in a garden, bending, hoeing, weeding. But I wonder at the longing because, this, what I'm doing right now, fills that picture. At this moment, I know I have all I want. The sun glimmering on spider webs woven through chicken wire enclosing the still fertile soil where my father planted onions and Swiss chard now covered with wild oats and star thistle turned pale at the end of summer.

Morning fresh smells of grass and dew, the sound of water escaping from sprinkler heads, an oak limb branching out hung with a grey, worn rope dangling against the sky. Next to the garden Daddy had built a small greenhouse of clear plastic sheeting which over the past 20 years has turned a creamy white while rampant grape vines etched themselves along its foundation. Makeshift water faucets rise from an assortment of pipes no longer carrying water. Grey wooden, leaning fence post of varying sizes support the bowed chicken wire. Tumbled in a corner lay rolled pieces of heavier wire that once entrapped tangled tomato vines to keep them from flowing over the soil where their red-ripe fruit would not.

I tell myself, "If I could describe heaven, this is what it would be." And tears flood my eyes. I don't know why, but the longing – the lonely pull deep inside goes. I feel I've weeded the garden, I'm a part of it, and all around me is a friend. This scene of green grape leaves and cream colored plastic, grey brown rotting posts, pale wheat colored weeds and grasses, shadowed oak branches sparkled chicken wire and spun glass webs, the feel, sound, smell is permanent no matter how overgrown or unused it becomes.

I feel like someone who's wandered over pastures and fields, through woods and stumbled across an old homestead where time can be etched in a moment of feeling when your eyes, whole self-catches a sense of what used to be, what could have been. And I know, maybe, that's where my longing has come from. I've not had a garden in my life. I've moved on, away from the Earth's fertile soil, now I am back.

About the Author

Mary Ann Bachman grew up in the small Northern California town of Lincoln. She and her husband Lowell Kollenberg raised three children. Mary Ann spent most of her adult life working in the field of education.

After graduating from Sierra College with an AA she went on to earned a Bachelor of Science in Environmental

Protection and Management from the University California at Davis and a Bachelor of Science Vocational Education from the California State University Sacramento.

One of her goals in life was to volunteer for US Peace Corps. In1992 at the age of 58 this became a reality. She spent two years as a Peace Corp Volunteer working with other volunteers, the

local government and community groups on the Island of Dominica in the Eastern Caribbean. Currently Mary Ann resides in Lincoln where she spends a lot of time with her children and grand-children. She turned 80 years old in April 2015.

Printed in the United States
By Bookmasters